To Speed the Plough

To Speed the Plough

Mechanisation comes to the Farm

IAN NIALL

HEINEMANN : LONDON

William Heinemann Ltd
15 Queen Street, Mayfair, London W1X 8BE

LONDON   MELBOURNE   TORONTO
JOHANNESBURG   AUCKLAND

First published 1977
© Ian Niall 1977

SBN 434 51024 6

Printed and bound in Great Britain by
Butler & Tanner Ltd, Frome and London

Contents

With sixteen illustrations by C. F. Tunnicliffe

Introduction

WHEN I told my publisher of my plans for a book about the change in the countryside and the effect of the agricultural revolution, which is really a delayed phase of the industrial revolution of the seventeenth–eighteenth century, he was prompted to caution me to avoid a suggestion that the old ways were patently the best. I could, he thought, be indulging in nostalgia. I must say that it was just possible that this could have happened for I have a great self-indulgence in looking at what seems to be a romantic world existing somewhere in the early eighteenth century. I live in the world of men who were old when I was a child. I hear the corncrake. I see the haywain on the meadow and the corn being threshed with a flail, which is something my great-grandfather told me about when I was a very small boy.

I am, however, blessed or cursed with a streak of realism. I see the way the world goes, the inevitable course of things no politician can hope to alter, any more than an ant can get in the way of an elephant. To be truthful I never set out to produce a rural ride. If I had started on a pony I should have had to get down from its back before very long to complete the journey on an express train. The world contracts. Time is losing its meaning, both in terms of a day's work and distance travelled. Three parts of this book are about the different aspects of evolution affecting life in the country until the 'horsepower' age followed the age of the horse. It is possible to deal with the phases of change in transport, animal husbandry, cultivation up to the first three or four decades of this century. After that a proper study of the subject would call for much more specialized research, technical knowledge only individual specialists can possess. My conclusion is that we can tell where we have been if we stand still long enough to discover where we are. No one can say with certainty where we are going!

1

The Horse that Ran Off

THE BOOK of Genesis had to be written, I suppose, because man's life, and most of his experience, has beginning and end. There had to be a beginning. Charles Darwin and others with a deeper conception of life produced another theory that really embraced no beginning and no ending. Nevertheless, accounting for things as they now are requires a degree of back-tracking. Man evolved the use of the wheel and the principles of leverage and no one took note of the exact date or even the century, but everything began to roll with the wheel. It only called for the lash to hurry it all along. The ox was stronger than a dozen slaves although the powerful beast needed the goad. It was a long, long haul before the working horse, derived from the horse of war, really took the place of the ox. If one picks as one's subject the progress of modern agriculture one must first contemplate a leisurely journey through centuries in which communication and the spread of knowledge was slow. Peaceful exchanges between peoples were much less common than violent ones and it is hard indeed to say where and when progress became apparent. The professional historian has the answer in a case like this. He picks his beginning and interprets in terms of ages or periods of measured time. He uses a slab out of the middle. History is really about revolution and the subject is much too big for any one historian, even a Gibbon. If what is happening to us, a breeding-up race of men, the inheritors of all the ages, stone, bronze, iron, steam and atomic, is truly revolution we must face the fact that 'progress' doesn't necessarily imply improvement. We misuse the word progress. In agricultural Britain we were once an entirely peasant community and had work for many hands. Progress

dispensed with the hands and the 'hands' went off to breed a generation of town-dwellers all needing to be fed, all without the skills
of their ancestors but all depending on the land as much as ever.
The most significant event in the past fifty years so far as life on
the land is concerned was the passing of the day of the working
horse. It is what led up to it and what has arisen since that fasci-
nates me and seems as awe-inspiring as the first landing on the
moon. It was certainly something with more immediate effect on
millions of people than the most sophisticated ironmongery being
boosted into lunar orbit.

Once when I was a child, in a world in which all horses seemed
at least eighteen hands high and men almost as tall, I was taken
by my farmer elders to what we called a cattle show. There, with
my hand tightly held in that of an uncle or aunt (I forget which)
I peered through hurdles and under rails to see what could be seen.
It was a world of horses, not just high-stepping trotters and jaunty
little ponies in gigs and governess carts but enormous Clydesdales.
The grass of the field was trodden to a kind of green juicy pulp
by a pedestrian people who wore homespun tweeds and boots and
cloth caps. They knew little of the motor car except that it was a
noisy, fuming nuisance. The word pollution hadn't been culled
from the dictionary as yet, but there was nothing wrong with our
noses. The sickly sweet smell of vaporized petrol was unnatural.
Horse dung had a bearable odour. Some people actually liked it.
It was while I was turning away from the rails of the show field
that it happened. All at once there was a shout from the crowd,
a staggering and falling back to give way before a terror-stricken
harness horse that had set its ears flat on its head and showed the
whites of its eyes as it plunged forward. At the extremity of the
horse's leathers, with his leg tightly entangled in them, was an unfortunate horseman who was dragged along and was in imminent
danger of having his brains knocked out. A harness horse was lighter
than a draught horse, a well-groomed, spirited animal as a rule,
capable of doing his proud owner justice when he bowled along to
church or went visiting. This particular horse was one such. His
nostrils flared. Foam flecked on his mouth. He snorted his excitement and his hooves cut the turf and sent chunks of moist earth into
the air as he hammered his way along. The man at the end of the

leathers seemed to be set upon his last journey. If he travelled behind a horse again it would be one with black plumes and mourning drapery. Just before I was hauled out of the way I saw a man dash forward and grab the rein to add his weight to the runaway's burden, while other men, less brave, blasphemed or sat on the rails with their mouths gaping. The second man must have been paring his tobacco with a knife at the moment the horse came on the scene for he was able to cut the leathers and free the entangled victim of the runaway. The horse went on, however. The crowd parted and stumbled and staggered to avoid being trampled under its feet and then they closed in again. I could hear the cries of alarm as the horse went on. The two men who were sprawled on the grass were quickly helped to their feet and revived with a pull from a whisky bottle. I wondered if anyone ever would stop that horse before it reached the blue hills that were the limit of my child's world.

This brief, horrifying encounter with the runaway had an equally horrifying sequel for me. I was put to bed on my return home, weary and exhausted and perhaps slightly sick from too much of the marvellous Italian ice cream which one could always buy at cattle shows and fêtes in those days. I awoke screaming in the middle of the night. I had had a nightmare in which I was tied at the end of a rein and towed away by a wild horse with foam flying from its mouth. The horse couldn't be stopped. Drunken men clutched at one another and stopped with bottles half-raised to their lips. No one rushed out of the crowd to cut the rein. The runaway never stopped. The horror was real and it was a long time before I was comforted and persuaded to close my eyes again. Now, embarking upon a book which is about the horse and horsepower, largely the story of a runaway, I wonder if I might entitle it The Horse That Ran Off. In the ordinary course of events horses ran off every day. They got bitten on the tender underbelly by a rainfly. They got frightened by a car or a steam traction engine. They would shy at a shadow. I had seen it often— a binder bouncing like a Roman chariot and flails turning like a windmill in a storm—a milkcart with lids jangling and milk running under the tailboard as the horse went into a gallop, losing his cool. I saw the intrusion of the steam engine and the internal combustion engine without being aware that the industrial revolution had ever started. Indeed, I wasn't aware of the loom and all the other mechanical wonders that the revolution had brought. Peasant farming was really an insignificant industry if anyone called it industry but it had been backed for hundreds of years by corn laws governing the price of bread and corn in the cornmarkets. The revolution's backwash of mechanical advancement brought first a corn reaper to put mowers with scythes out of work and then a flail reaper and finally McCormick's binder. At this stage no one realized that farming would become more and more a matter of capital investment. It wouldn't do to recruit the family and then the children of the cottager and perhaps half the children of the village, for they wouldn't be able to achieve in a month what would eventually have to be done in a day. The flail reaper and the modern binder were horse-drawn, of course. We had always walked before we ran and we had a lot of things we had to weigh up and consider before we abandoned them. There was, for instance, the threshing machine and the steam plough. The steam plough was only of limited usefulness. It had to be hauled or haul itself along the headland to winch in the plough on its cable. Steam hadn't been the answer either when it came to ploughing or reaping but it remained the answer when it came to threshing grain. The threshing floor and the hand flails had been put out of action. Like the scythe they would be curiosities. The horse remained the king-pin of organized cultivation, ploughing, reaping and mowing. We would soon rush headlong into a new age, however. The horse would run away. It would never stop. We already had a new measure of energy and farmers would begin to use the word coined for them—horsepower. Nothing would slow us down once it all began to roll, except the final intervention of a non-agrarian race—the Arabs—who had once loved horses but by this time would have abandoned both the horse and the camel for the shiny product of Detroit equipped with powered steering and air conditioning.

It is very easy when one belongs to a particular generation to look at what has been with nostalgia. The scenes of my childhood hark back to the scenes painted by Constable, Millais and Turner. The world then, if one takes the work of the artist for real, was shaded by tall elms, watered by gently flowing streams and green-weeded ponds. Great haywains trundled gently across pastures or stubbles.

This is the world as one would have had it, not exactly as it was! I too, have mental pictures that emphasize what was idyllic and eliminates what was probably not so pleasant. I recall a world in which I rode home high on the neck of a working horse still with all the trappings of his harness draped on him. It was a world in which we lay back on grassy banks to drink tea from bowls and eat jam-covered scones while the hay waited to be turned, butterflies fluttered about us and grasshoppers sang. There it all is, running through my mind, a silent film of the hot summers of long ago, or of the brilliant light of the spring sky with plovers flying above the harrowed earth. My grandmother spent all her time, I can believe, baking scones or stirring fruit in a preserving pan. My aunts always had baskets of brown eggs on their arms or came with slabs of newly-made butter from the dairy. We sang at the piano. The porridge pot bubbled. We had wonderful suppers on Sunday. We were always having picnics on the shore. In winter the background to life was the call of the wintering greylags. If the wind made the fire smoke it wasn't the acrid smell of burning coal but the wonderful scent of peat. No one in that world, if you choose to believe me, had rheumatism or a lung-searing cough that wouldn't respond to goose grease, brown paper, camphorated oil, or Ellerman's horse oil, made from soft soap and turpentine I always thought. Only under pressure would I admit that hacked hands bled. My poor grandmother was nearly killed when she was kicked in the ribs by a cow and the milk often went sour on a hot summer morning when we couldn't get it to the creamery on time. With all the power of nostalgia—a word for which the Greeks needed two, and a sickness to which I am often prone—I see the sower walking the field like a soldier, up and down, every pace the same. It happened in my time and owes nothing to Millet or the story of Ruth and Naomi toiling in the harvest field of Boaz. Peats were cut in my time, away on the myrtle-scented moss, and dried there by the summer winds to make them fit for stacking and burning in winter hearths. To counter-balance such flights of poetic description I must add that lifting swedes on a freezing, wet November day was a kind of purgatory, an experience only comparable to service in the salt mines. If meadowsweet and honeysuckle perfumed the evening air one understood why there had to be such delights in a world where a man ran barrows up a slippery midden plank to 'muck out' pigs.

These were not the good old days, because the good old days never existed until they were winnowed out from the whole crop of days, like good corn winnowed from the chaff of weeds and thorns. Old men looked back and expressed wonder at how the world had changed but then I was too young to appreciate what they meant. Railways had criss-crossed the country in my father's and grandfather's day. When I was born the steam traction engine had come crawling up the road to make our built-in threshing mill, a walk mill powered by a single horse, obsolete, although we still used it. The threshing mill was one of the wonders of my world because it had glamour as well as power. The engine radiated heat. It was all brass and levers and great heavy drive wheels. It didn't run on rails but came slowly, grinding its way over the stone-metalled road and telling the countryside that it was on the move. It smoked and chuffed and rumbled and its driver had to spin a steering wheel with frantic haste when he wanted the short train to make an abrupt turn. This was the final lunge of the steam age. I recognize it now for what it was, but I didn't see the internal combustion engine making it, and the working horse, redundant. No one would want to scrap such a grand piece of machinery with its shining brass and its hot coals spilling from its ashbox while sparks sailed in the evening air to drive off midges and warn bats to keep clear. Even this clumsy train was a long way from Stephenson and his Rocket and men like him who had toiled and toyed with condensers and turbines. I am sure that neither Watt nor Newcomen who had studied the work of Savery had ever contemplated ploughing a field or threshing a field of corn with steam. In 1698 when Savery was plotting the practical possibilities of a steam engine most people considered steam to be the useless by-product of a boiling kettle. To tell the truth steam was to be a great disappointment. We had to have done with it, along with the penny-farthing bicycle!

The good old days weren't even those when a schooner of beer cost a halfpenny because even when it did, and that was long before I was born, beer had to be cheap. Men needed to drown their sorrows when labour was engaged at the hiring fair and farmers prodded potential employees to see if they had enough muscle on them to do what had to be done. A man had to be almost as strong as the working horse with which his sweat mingled. They harrowed furrows together in a duststorm and they broke the lea with the plough even when the ground was iron hard. When something did come to alleviate their misery it would banish the most intelligent animal ever to serve man and make the man a machine-minder, like almost everyone already affected by the industrial revolution. Change was taking place but the last people to be ultimately affected by the nineteenth-century revolution were as unconscious of its happening as Mesmer's patients. If they ever came out of their trance they would swear it had all come about overnight. The wheel had really begun to turn in the middle of the nineteenth century. The vehicle had begun to gain momentum. It would run easily because of a principle which the engineer called traction, all tied up with weight and the overcoming of inertia. Salesmen would sell the word, or one very like it, listing its horsepower and pointing out that when it was stabled it didn't eat oats. It needed very little grooming and it wasn't hard to catch even although it might be harder to start than a pair of Shires or a Clydesdale.

In the old days of peasant agriculture, when men and horses were to be had for very little money, such change as there was had come from men like Turnip Townsend, who was far ahead of his time in more than one respect, although he is a forgotten man now. Turnip Townsend looked at the amount of seed he had to sow to grow turnips and the unsatisfactory way in which the crop grew, here, there and everywhere, and sometimes leaving the field with bare patches like a moth-eaten carpet. Not only was it difficult to lift the crop in any reasonable way to make sure it was all of a size and quality for putting in store or clamp, but weeds grew among it and the turnips that were over thickly sown were all leaf and no root. Turnip Townsend invented the turnip drill and he was away because the drill could sow the seed in rows, spilling it in a trickle from a set of little hoppers. A horse could pull the drill. Where there had been chaos and disorder there was a pattern of workable rows, rows from which the unwanted plants could be singled or thinned, rows which could be weeded and kept tidy and from which the turnips could be lifted and piled in the wagon without as much as one being crushed by the wheels. Until Townsend's brilliant idea the turnip had depended upon the broadcasting hand of the sower and turnip seed, being small and round, is probably the most difficult of all seeds to sow broadcast. Townsend solved a problem and made another, which is what inevitably happens when someone thinks he makes progress. Labourers of some kind had to be employed to 'single' the turnips and pull the weeds. There was really no great problem here so long as Townsend and his imitators could persuade the children of the district to work in the fields, crawling on hands and knees and thinning out the turnips as they went up and down the rows. Children won't work with any great enthusiasm for very long unless they are supervised. There had to be a gang master or mistress to keep them at it. Although Townsend had no idea of the evil he was creating, and may not have cared had it been pointed out, someone finally had to regulate the thinning of rows and indeed the harvesting of crops by young persons. Finally an Act of Parliament had to be passed to prevent exploitation of the children by unscrupulous gang masters who hired their recruits to anyone who could use them, making them little better than slaves.

When he had solved the problem of the turnip's cultivation Turnip Townsend might have thought about the corn drill. If he did he was incapable of finding a man who knew how to devise a machine to scatter grain in the way that the sower did. Instead of concentrating on a mechanical problem Townsend gave thought to the land and how it could be induced to give the best yield of root or grain. He 'invented' four-year crop rotation. Almost two hundred and fifty years afterwards we are in need of being reminded of the sound principle of resting land before we exhaust it, for today, greedy for the current price of potatoes or grain, there are many farmers who ignore what Townsend discovered, that even in the rich loam of Norfolk and the Fens, a crop repeated too often will leave the land unable to produce a worthwhile yield. In Townsend's day his theory wasn't accepted on all sides. Indeed a gentleman set out to prove that this was nonsense and grew wheat on the same land for thirteen years, increasing the yield every year it is said. With places in which there was as much as twenty or thirty feet of silt deposit and humus beneath a farmer's feet it was possible to prove almost anything, although eelworm in potatoes and rust in wheat ultimately guarantee that the law of diminishing returns must apply. For a hundred years after the turnip drill no one really solved the slow business of cutting hay or grain although many had tried. The mower mowed and the gleaner gleaned. When the sun blazed down for a month at harvest time everything went along at a satisfactory pace. There were enough people to serve the mower, to turn the hay, to rake it and turn it time and time again, and to soldier on into the golden evenings of autumn when shadows were long and the first frost wasn't far off. This is the way it had all been since the days of the Old Testament. If there had been anything invented of particular note it had been the iron plough to replace the old one made of wood and drawn by man himself, or his ox. The iron age bred mechanics however. Da Vinci had given everyone a principle for whatever problem lay before them. The gunsmith concentrated on fine mechanisms and the man standing at the weaver's elbow carefully studied what hands and crude shuttles could accomplish. In a strange way the solution to the harvesting problem was evolved by men who probably had never stood in a harvest field. The twine-knotter was an inspiration. So far as the farmer was concerned it was the work of genius, no less.

Without talking about the knotter, which made the corn binder the first mechanical monster to work in the field, here in fact was the death knell of a thousand craftsmen, the depopulation of rural areas, the banishing of the corncrake as well as thousands of horses. Nothing apparently happens in a lifetime until one looks closely at it, nothing that is, except perhaps an atomic bomb or a flight out to the far-off stars. In my childhood I heard the corncrake every summer's night. I even found its nest in the long grass of the hayfield and shot one as it rose ahead of me and hurried away, although I was dismayed to discover what I had done. I drove a horse binder with a team of three and then five Clydesdales. Don't ask me how a boy operates a machine balanced on one broad wheel and one spindly wheel six feet or more away from it, and controls not three but five animals weighing a ton or almost a ton each, and with enough power to move a mountain. In the horse age this was no wonder. It was what had to be done and all that the horseman needed to know were the words of command, hup, high and whoa there! The thing would roll away at great speed. The corn would topple under the rolling flails and quickly rise on the sheets of canvas

that conveyed it to be gathered in the sheaf, looped round its circumference with hairy twine, and the twine knotted and cut beyond the
knot before it was tossed on to the stubble. This happened as fast
as the horses could plod. All at once the man on the machine became
part of the mechanical process, operating a lever now and again,
touching the mare's rump with the long binderwhip as flexible as
the fly fisherman's rod, and feeling like a sailor on a golden, rippling
sea that was ripe corn. The man who made this possible was by
no stretch of imagination a farmer or a peasant. Whatever he called
himself he was an engineer. His part in it was very small. On the
great plains of America they would harness ten or twenty horses
to bigger and wider cutting binders. At least once they would create
a record and have thirty horses all pulling the same machine and
then, thinking how things might be done more economically with
fewer horses, they would hitch a normal team to a binder and follow
one binder with another, two, three, four. No one asked what the
next step was to be but already McCormick's binder was to be modified into a combine and hauled by giant tractor until the whole
thing could be incorporated into one and the thirty horse teams sent
to the knacker's yard.

It is hard not to be sentimental about the horse when one has
worked alongside it, felt the warmth of its body, comforted it when
it has fallen and come to grief, seen how it will respond to a
whispered word and discovered that some horses have a sense of
humour where man may have little. Man began to exploit the horse
from the moment he first clawed his way on to its ungroomed back
and managed to stay there. It is certain that he flogged it and used
it cruelly, but time taught him that a good horse is as good as a good
man and the horse is an animal that responds quicker to kindness
than to the whip. What was asked of the horse from which the working strain was evolved was obedience and steadfastness in the uproar
of the charge when lances tilted men from the saddle and axes split
their skulls. This war horse was heavy and more inclined to canter
than to trot. It knew the name of the game. It shouldered its
opponent and used its weight. It turned at the touch of its master's
knees. It responded to his spurs and if it lived long enough he bred
others from it. It was the tank of its day. A thousand horses could
topple a kingdom. The Romans had ridden them to conquer all

Gaul. The work horse at this time was a light, not very well bred
nag lacking the sheer hauling power of the ox, but soon the blood
of war horses was introduced to this lesser breed to give them bone
and muscle to take over the plough. This was where it really began,
the age of the working horse. It ended in my generation. My grandfather, who was a blacksmith before he farmed and not unsuccessful
at his trade, inventing agricultural implements, insisted that his son
stay away from the smithy. He would have nothing to do with making him apprentice to his own trade. The trade was doomed he said.
This was just after the turn of the century. The tractor and the combine harvester were still a long way off. The trade of blacksmith
wasn't doomed of course. It would survive when the working horse
was extinct but the arrival of the corn binder had opened the old
man's eyes to the shape of things to come. He had quickly acquired
the mechanical skill to keep the McCormick binder and the Albion
working in the harvest field despite their breakdowns. He somehow
knew that it wouldn't be very long before someone hitched the
mechanical harvester to a mechanical horse. When he farmed he
kept a stable of Clydesdales and ploughed at least two teams, carting
with six or seven animals at harvest time. There was no abrupt end
to the day of the working horse. It didn't happen like Hiroshima.
All at once someone noticed that the horse binder wasn't out there
any more. In its place was a tractor pulling the machine. In time
they might notice that there were no people on the field and a lonely
man sat high on the combine driving it like a long distance lorry.
They eventually noticed that there were only two or three teams in
competition at the horse ploughing match. There weren't any old
ploughmen to compete. Time is money, farmers were saying, and
if no one can control the weather the only solution is to plough faster
and harvest quicker. A horse needed to be tended by a blacksmith
and a vet if it shed a shoe or took colic. A tractor needed only a
mechanic and he could delve into its intestines and replace its vital
organs, even if he couldn't stop the whole from wearing out. A
written-off tractor could still do something given a gallon of kero-
sene. A written-off horse was another matter. The knacker would
probably want to be paid for carting it away.

    The horse took off, nevertheless. Its output had been measured
and translated into foot pounds or whatever the expert in mechanics

chose to call it. Its ghost haunted the lump of cast iron with the atomizer and the battery. Mr Ford and Mr Ferguson did everything they could to make man forget that he had once talked to his horse. The best way they could find to do that was to give him more horses than he knew what to do with. They gave him more ploughs to turn furrows, more discs, more harrows. They made him look back at what he had ploughed instead of forward to see if the line horse was holding straight. They trundled him and his ploughs over acre after acre, rattling his bones in the process, sometimes doing more in a day than he had hitherto done in a month. They built him a little cabin in which he could travel. They even gave him headlights by which he could work at night and when he had it all he had no hankering to go back to the long walk from autumn into spring in the company of gulls and through the flights of nesting plovers. Alas, we are in a generation that no longer recognizes even the ghost of the working horse and has accepted horsepower as a number, a cc rating based on the bore of a cylinder. The horse doesn't come into it at all. The truth is it never did. Horsepower was notional. It could never have been anything else and 'brake' horsepower was coined to heap confusion upon confusion.

2

To Plough

THE PLOUGH is surely the only invention of man to have been delineated for him in the pattern of the stars. The ancients of Greece had seen only birds and animals in the backcloth of the night sky, bears and doves to which they gave names. The man whose lot it was to plough was not a scholar but a peasant concerned with his survival rather than the appeasement of gods and the extension of philosophy. If he looked to the heavens he was work-weary. If he asked for anything it was the strength to hold the crudely fashioned wooden implement that was little more than the trunk of a tree which his son or his wife hauled. He churned the hard dusty earth for centuries before the wooden implement was refined in iron and if he at last recognized the iron plough for what it was, he must have marvelled at the fact that it had been there in the stars since the beginning of time. The wooden plough was used for centuries before this happened. Teams of ruminating oxen, eight powerful beasts might pull it and with it the peasant ploughed most of the arable land of Europe. Once it was fashioned in iron the pace changed. The iron plough glided through the rich loam, slipped through the moist earth and ironed it smoothly, furrow upon furrow. The wooden plough could never make such furrows. The peasant must have been delighted with this greatly improved implement.

There were ploughs and ploughs, of course, and some ploughmakers had more imagination than others, more nous, a better appreciation of the way a thing might be done. Land is not everywhere the same and imagination is what gives mankind the implements he needs. The makers of ploughs met their problems quite

literally where they stood and made their ploughs to turn that particular ground. In one place land is deep and heavy and in another
light and easily washed away by the storm. In the rich earth of the
Fens of England a heavy plough might sail steadily along like a gal-
lean ploughing across the Atlantic; but it was not so everywhere and
the plough to turn the scrubland of the hilly north or west was a
very different kind of vessel. In the treacherous rocks of wilder parts
the lighter plough would pitch and roll and come to grief. It wal-
lowed in deeps and the man at the stilts looked critically at its shape
and weight when he ran aground and broke its bowsprit. He suffered
more than callouses. His ribs were bruised when the plough
foundered.

Despite the craft of artificers in metal it was never going to be
easy to plough with a horse plough because it involved such essentially physical elements—the use of an iron implement pulled by a
horse and held by a man. If anything should have inspired further
invention it was this painful labour but the drawback to inspiration
was that the man at the plough was not an inventor or a worker
in metal. He ploughed alone. His suffering was personal and un-
witnessed out there on the lonely hill or the flat plain. Galley slaves
and the labourers scourged to build a temple might find common
cause but the peasant's suffering was in the first instance self-in-
flicted. He had the choice of ploughing or starving and compared
with what had gone before the iron plough must have seemed a godsend. Ploughing was, however, a business to make a philosopher
of a thinking man and the ploughman must have concluded that
there was no help for it but the passing of days in bondage. He did
this staggering with one leg down in the furrow and the other up
on the land for days without end knowing that there was no help
for it and he must steer a straight course or all his labour would
be in vain. When the plough came to grief on a rock the blacksmith
mended it. He re-forged the point of the ploughshare. The 'sock'
was generally made of self-sharpening material (in later days a car-
bonized mild steel) but when the point really wore away the smith
could bring it to a white heat and beat it out once more, renewing
it as long as enough material remained to enable him to do so. This
was the only wear and tear in the business of ploughing except the
long-drawn agony of men and horses. Even the team and the

ploughman himself were hardened in the fire. They had to be hardened for they were on a long walk that took them more than half a year. Turning the stubble of a previous harvest was easy for the land was like a well-cultivated garden and rolled off the mouldboard like soft cheese. Lea ploughing was a very different matter. There was concentrated misery in it. A man's muscles never ceased to be under strain. His shoulders grew weary and his back would become hunched as he held the plough in the ground. The hooves of horses, cows or sheep would have hammered the pasture. The wheels of wagons and carts consolidated it as they passed from one field to another. In places it was as hard as the old farm road. This kind of ploughing was not for an apprentice or a gangling youth with half-developed muscles and spindly limbs. It tested a strong man. It put a weakling on his back while the season went on.

The purpose of ploughing and its usefulness is debated nowadays when there is controversy and so many new ideas about how we should use and manage the land. There are many people who now ask why we plough and if we ever needed to. In the day of the horse plough many a man must have wondered about the necessity of turning so much land. The plough was designed to turn the turf over. Doing just this it enriches the soil in which the crop is to grow because the grass and its roots compost down. The soil needs this humus improvement, the composting not only of grass or stubble but the aftergrowth of weeds. The land is aerated and the balance of moisture is adjusted by evaporation and by the improvement in surface drainage. The old ploughman would have said that if the plough wasn't needed it was a strange thing that weeds always outnumbered edible plants and corn never grew of its own accord. If the plough was obsolete worms and moles were redundant. They also aerate the soil. Leaving so much to nature the chances are that man would starve. He must invest his labour and do all he can to adjust the balance in his favour. Theories are all very well but they rarely put food in the mouth very quickly. Great nations with no shortage of experts to produce theories have faced disaster at harvest time through cultivating theory. Few ploughmen seriously questioned the need to plough any more than trawlermen question the need to fish in the icy waste of northern seas. Most ploughmen following a team staggered on into driving rain and faced the misery of hail and sleet without asking why. The inventors and modifiers of ploughs had brought the horse plough to perfection. There was no further refinement that could be made. What had they done? They had given the plough coulters to part the turf and split the sod, a share to cut the furrow, a mouldboard to lay that furrow, a landwheel to balance the implement on one side and a furrow wheel on the other. A man could work out how many days, weeks or months of ploughing lay before him by ploughing his first furrow and then pacing his field—roughly three furrows to the yard. Give or take a few days he knew the time his walk would take. He walked like the sower or the shepherd not to count minutes, hours or days, but to get to the end of what had to be done. It took that kind of outlook. A man who had any other would have given up or been destroyed by the magnitude of his task. A ploughman ploughed each day and tomorrow wasn't even a dream or it could have become a nightmare.

In terms of achievement a furrow meant a distance varying from nine to fifteen inches in width, ploughed two or three inches deep on the poorest land to more than six inches in rich loam. The design of plough and the setting governed the width of the furrow. The depth was achieved by the adjustment of coulters and wheels. On level ground free of hidden rocks and boulders ploughing might proceed at a steady pace. This was the pace of a pair of Shire or Clydesdale horses. The team would always be well-matched. They would set their own pace without being goaded or urged along. The team would be well-used to working in double harness. The line horse, on which the ploughman relies to steer an even course, was a special animal that never deviated or pulled off. Having cut the first furrow it walked the headland to make the second and the commands needed to keep it under control were 'hup, high and whoa!' but the lines could be tied to the plough handles. The line horse needed few reprimands or instructions. The ploughman devoted his energies to holding the plough at an even depth. The mouldboard pared the furrow and often a supplementary iron called a smoother, firmed it and left it polished. While the ploughman ploughed, gulls would sail behind him or drop to snatch up worms and grubs. Lazy hares would rise and leisurely lope away. The newly turned earth would steam in the morning sunlight and partridges make their slow way across the path of the team as untroubled as farmyard birds. In spring the ploughman would often halt his team and move the nest of the plover to one side, replacing the eggs in a hollow after the plough had passed. He was involved with nature and the creatures of his field and he was generally the most important man on the farm. In the scheme of things he would either have a tied cottage or live in. He was paid a little more not for the hardship of his work but for his skill and earned perhaps a shilling or two a week more than a stockman. He knew his worth at the fair and stood with others of his calling, a class of man above the common run of men. He often found an employer on the strength of his reputation as a good ploughman. Good men were always hard to come by and the whole process of arable farming depended upon a farmer finding a man who could plough well.

What ultimately happens to ploughing may seem to make nonsense of the perfectly straight furrow but there was a purpose in the even pattern achieved by the ploughman and his team. Cultivation by the furrow plough always moves land, transports soil in one direction or another. This in fact applies to the man who digs a garden, for if turf is taken off in order to get down to the business of digging, the soil is not just deprived of humus, the landscape is altered by the piling up of turf or sods. The horse plough and the system in which it was employed ensured the preservation of the even contour of the land, preventing soil from piling up in ditches, slowly crumbling and washing downhill and exposing not only subsoil but bedrock which is in effect erosion. There was more to the ploughman's insistence upon regularity and order than just pleasing the eye. A man didn't simply come to the plough but needed to be taught what ploughing was about. He served his time to ploughing whether he was apprenticed or not and ploughmen never were. The old horse plough has become a curiosity, a bygone for the pub yard or the country cottage garden. It generally escapes the eye of the casual observer that the single furrow plough is 'handed'. It throws a furrow to the right hand, having one ploughshare, one mouldboard. A plough driven up a field and immediately back down it to lay a second furrow in line with the first would make a kind of ditch or depression and if this continued across the field the result would be a series of such wallows, a ditch every twenty or thirty

inches from one side of the field to the other. However the final
harrowing was done this would produce a shambles rather like the
rooting of a herd of pigs. No amount of harrowing and rolling could
restore the field to its original state. The horse plough was never
set to plough haphazardly. It hadn't a reversible mouldboard like
the modern, multiple ploughs hauled by the tractor. There was no
way of overcoming the fact that it was 'handed' except by ploughing
to a measured pattern. This was done by ploughing up and ploughing down at a measured distance apart—roughly five and a half yards
to the left hand and five and a half to the right hand, the 'gathering'
being eleven yards. This resulted in strips of ploughing generally
called rigs. To ensure this pattern the plough would be eased
out of the furrow at the headland and slid along it to be entered
again on the way back down again. At the extremity of the rig the
total movement along the headland would be eleven yards. Two
poles (rig poles) make one chain of ploughing. A furlong—twenty-
two chains—would contain an area of ten acres or 48,400 square
yards. Sliding the plough on the headland prevented a slough
developing between the end of the furrow and the hedge or
ditch. When the whole field had been ploughed the team
would be set to ploughing the headland either outwards on an
anticlockwise circuit or inwards on a clockwise direction according to the need to keep the soil moving in one direction or the
other.

A well-trained and well-matched plough team didn't need to be
told to wheel and move along the headland. The ploughman only
needed to turn his plough on to its side and they would throw themselves into their collars and stamp along to turn in again. Occasionally the ploughman, hurrying after them would plant his foot on
the plough handles to prevent the ploughshare digging in. The
movement became automatic. The plough team were like circus
horses performing in the ring but of course there was a great deal
more to it when the plough was set to the lea. Here the land was
being turned for the first time in several years perhaps. As like as
not there remained not a trace of previous ploughing pattern. Land
long lying fallow may show no sign of ever having been turned
before. There needed to be guidelines, markers to steer by. The
rig pole was used to mark the field so that the 'scratch furrows' could

be made. This shallow furrow is not only a guide but supports the first furrow cut by the single furrow plough. A two-mouldboard plough was sometimes used to make scratches. This plough was a somewhat versatile implement though it couldn't be used for proper ploughing. It was sometimes called a hiller because it made 'hills' or earthed up rows. It was also used for splitting the rows and sometimes for discouraging weeds between rows. It was invaluable to the man who after ploughing in the ordinary way wanted a crop of potatoes. It became obsolete as a potato digger when the mechanical digger with a pole or shafts came on the scene. Its plough frame no doubt inspired the drill harrow which was fitted with a set of teeth to churn the weeds from the place between ridges.

The hiller was by no means the only modification of the horse plough. Plough-makers were great individualists, whatever the industrial revolution was doing to those who worked towards mechanization and mass production. They might not be able to take the backache out of ploughing but they studied the plough and consulted the man who was ploughing. They were mechanics of the same kind as those studying the steam engine, the principle of internal combustion and so on. Ahead of their time some of them thought to get rid of the horse by using the steam engine. There had been a few double frame ploughs, ploughs that, with extra horsepower could plough two furrows instead of one. The double-framed steam plough seemed to have a lot to recommend it and one was produced without trouble. It depended on hawsers or cables, of course. The steam engine couldn't be allowed to tear the soil from the rock by travelling up and down the field. It was just the thing for good level land, the inventors said, and they were right. It did well on level land. It was no use on hilly ground and most of the arable land of this country is other than flat. Not only was there a complication in the winching of the plough from one end of the field to the other but the steam engine or engines occupied the headland along which they had to crawl to achieve the cultivation. The horse plough was a simple device. It ran on oats and needed no coal. It was reliable. There was hardly anything that could go wrong. Farming depended on the horse because steam couldn't do much about harvesting, carting or anything else without level ground. Single furrow ploughs had variety enough without anyone contriving to make them different. In different parts of the country the horse plough showed the variety of imagination. What a farmer or a ploughman asked for, the ploughmaker tried to do for him and ploughing with two horses was always going to be a matter of hand and eye. A man's agony could be reduced by skilful adjustment of the parts of a plough, taking up the links in a chain, lowering or raising a land-wheel, altering the rake of the sock.

The vital parts of the horse plough had different names in different parts of the country and to list them all would be no small task. A plough has more than a slight resemblance to a sailing boat. It runs heavily and makes slow progress without being trimmed for its voyage. The man at the helm holds the course and the perfect plough turns a perfect furrow when everything is just right. Standing behind his plough the ploughman looks down at the handles or stilts which curve downwards to the beam and the frame where they are held apart or are braced by ties of shorter and shorter length. The frame of the plough supports the mouldboard and the toe on which the 'sock' is hammered in place. The ploughshare or sock is detachable because it must be sharpened from time to time. The width of the ploughshare determines the width of the furrow. A share with a broad fin produces a wide furrow and the lie of the furrow is determined by the mouldboard. In lea ploughing and often for competition ploughing the mouldboard might sometimes be elliptical in shape with a gentle curve to produce a pleasing furrow. Lea ploughing, because the ground is always hard, needs to be more gently moulded or the plough will put too great a strain on both the ploughman and his team. While the depth of the furrow is determined by the adjustment of the wheels, the ploughman bears down or holds up the handles to maintain an even depth. Nothing would work without the coulter or coulters with which every horse plough is fitted. The main coulter runs in front of and a little above the ploughshare which is shaped not unlike a harpoon. The purpose of the share is to square the bottom of the furrow and lift the earth to the mouldboard. Before it can do this it needs to have the turf broken by a coulter known as a skim coulter. Both coulters can be adjusted for depth and to a slight degree for rake. Without them the plough would delve and root like a pig and quickly come to a standstill behind a mound of unbroken turf. The landwheel takes a little weight from both the ploughman and his team but an important adjustment is made at the 'tee' of the plough by means of the linkage. Even a perfectly matched team may not pull the same weight and any small difference in the direction of effort will have an effect on the ploughing. The 'tee' is an elipse of iron with a series of holes drilled in it to allow the angle of draught to be adjusted and balanced. Links in the coupling of draught chains may be taken up at the swingle tree to which the 'tee' is fastened. This evens the load on the horses. When the 'tee' is offset properly the pulling becomes smooth and the plough glides along. This doesn't mean that the old ploughman didn't have to change anything once he had adjusted the plough at the beginning; for heavy, light or very wet land would require some modifications and most fields would have hazards, hillocks, ancient boulders left by the movement of the glacier perhaps, and these would have to be taken into account and circumnavigated or skirted to complete a furrow.

It was at the ploughing match that such skills came into their own. An indifferent ploughman might obliterate some of his mistakes by going over the field a time or two with chain harrows when the time came. At a ploughing match a man came under the eye of critical spectators, old country characters who knew the business and had ploughed in their youth. To compete at a match the old-time ploughman would often disdain land or furrow wheels. His plough was streamlined to run smoothly and evenly with no more to keep it true than his hands on the stilts. He whispered to his team. Their ears flicked or barely moved in response to his words but they heard them and responded. Fields chosen for ploughing matches were always viewed critically by the old hands and those taking part in the competition, because it depended what the rig was like whether or not a man got in the prize money. There was a serious handicap in having to plough a stony tract of land where the smoothness of the furrow might be impaired by stones that wouldn't be ironed. When the plough moved off the ploughman's concentration was like a marksman's but often before he had gone many yards he halted his team to make adjustments to the plough. Often he had experts close at hand to give him advice on these adjustments. A smith was bound to be

among the onlookers and next to a champion ploughman there was
no one who knew more about the adjustment of ploughs than a man
who made them. The plough had to cut the furrow like a moist
paring of cheese and leave it ironed to perfection, each furrow
against the previous one and every one identical and as straight as
a round rush. Competitions were usually local affairs. A ploughman couldn't move far beyond his own parish because his plough
had to be transported, on a cart perhaps, with the team in tow. A
competition would take up most of the day and almost invariably
the competitor would be ploughing on his master's land the day
afterwards. A champion ploughman became almost as famous as
a champion wrestler. His fame spread across the shire and fame
brought him a following that was strictly parochial and partisan.
The local man might be cheated out of his prize. He was never
beaten. A novice simply couldn't compete with a man who had won
for years because the champions and near champions had so much
experience. The top men won again and again until, at last, each in
turn went over the hill and lost their ability to handle the plough.
The beginner could hope for no shortcuts. The skill developed on
the long walk, miles and miles of furrows, year after year, time all
alone on the hill or in the seclusion of the meadow. When he began
to win he practised more and was encouraged by smiths and farmers.
He grew closer to his team and would remain with his employer
because of the team he ploughed. He loved his horses as much as
he loved the woman he married. He spent more time with them
than with his children. They were his audience when he sang. They
knew his moods. Sometimes they were the butt of his futile rage
when something went wrong but he would share his bread and jam
with them and lead them to shelter when an unbearable gale lashed
the land.

> Is my team ploughing
> That I used to drive
> And hear the harness jingle
> When I was man alive?

These were words Housman put into the mouth of the Shropshire
Lad. It is sometimes said that Housman had little more than fond
dreams of a west land he didn't know. He talked of blue remembered

hills and starlit fences but was far removed from the reality of a world he wrote about with such feeling. He was, in spite of his critics, uncannily aware of the affinity between a plough-man and his team. He knew the simplicity of peasant existence whether he had been in close contact with this kind of life or not.

> Ay the horses trample
> The harness jingles now
> No change though you lie under
> The land you used to plough.

No one was ever closer to the land than the man driving the plough and working with the animals that made cultivation possible. No one worked longer or harder to produce what the Bible promised the sower of seed—the tenfold yield to make bread. The ploughman's day was longer than most people's. It began before dawn. It ended after dark. The team was fed and groomed by the light of the storm lantern and watered after the ploughman had had his breakfast. He led them to the field with a raincoat hitched on the collar of one of them and as often as not their feet broke the ice on the puddles. He was at work by the time it was light enough to see half way across a mist-shrouded field. He expected a can of tea at mid-morning and crouched on his heels to drink it and eat his buttered bread. Even while he ate he remembered that when horses have raised a lather by their exertions they mustn't be left standing long or they will catch a chill on a cold day. Like humans they will fall sick. Like humans too, they have their little eccentricities. They become a team because they adapt one to the other and there is no way that a man can induce incompatible temperaments to work together. Every ploughman who had to replace one of a pair knew how impor-tant it was to make sure they were real stablemates. A young horse needed to be worked with an experienced line horse who would teach him the business the way an old sheepdog teaches a pup. The link between bridles or bits would draw the young horse round when they had to wheel on the headland. If as they ploughed the furrow he veered a little the old horse would stand firm and in the end they would both travel at the same steady pace, taking step for step and pulling their weight.

The long day was broken at noon when the team was unhitched to be taken back to the stable where they would be fed and watered, after which they went back to work until 'dropping' time when the chains were dropped and the team led clear of the plough. The ploughman walked between his horses, thankful for their support sometimes when he was near exhaustion and sheltered by their great shoulders. He removed their collars in the stable, fed them and sometimes groomed them before he had his supper. Before he went to bed he would look in on them again to see that they were settled, run a hand over their withers and console them in their fatigue, wishing perhaps that he might have been born with no more conception of tomorrow than they had. Their work began as soon as harvest was in and ricks were thatched. It was a point of honour to show the stubble being turned for this meant that work was well in hand. It was important not to be behind. Corn might not ripen all at once but there was no excuse for being late with the ploughing and the stubble could be easily turned. With the lea it was a different matter. It wasn't just that the field had to be marked out before ploughing could really begin. The lea ploughing needed to be broken by the frost. If the lea wasn't turned before the severe frosts set in it might be almost impossible to plough. When it was turned the hard frost broke the turf and helped to produce a degree of tilth which the harrows completed in spring. Beyond the urgency of getting a field turned before the weather brought ploughing to a standstill was the time of sowing in the spring. To be late with ploughing often meant being late with everything the following year.

A young ploughman took a pride in being able to plough the lea, sometimes called red land. He looked for a job as first ploughman and an increase in pay of a shilling or two a week. When he achieved recognition he would sit near the head of the table and be consulted about the work by his master. He took his washing home to his mother on a Sunday and didn't milk for he was a horseman at last. He was well enough fed but there was no overtime. He was engaged by the quarter or term and the bargain might include pocket money for beer and tobacco, so many flannel shirts, a pair of trousers and a pair of boots. He generally went for these to the draper in the nearest town, taking a signed chit which he handed to the shopman. His social life was almost non-existent. When the ploughing and harrowing and rolling were all done he carted, worked at hay and harvest. No one thought to call his a way of life. When he married or registered the birth of his children he put himself down as a farm servant.

3

The Sower and the Seed

MUCH LONGER than the walk of the ploughman behind oxen or horses was the walk of the sower. He had come out of the east when the western tribes were hunters or nomads. He was a mystical figure to attract the attention of the scribes. He was depicted on tombs. The corn they might cultivate in another existence was buried in the tombs of kings along with their armour. The very word corn was equated with life itself, with bread and water, years of plenty or of famine. The sower broadcast the corn of Egypt. He sowed wheat in England although in the less hospitable northern parts of Britain corn meant oats. To the layman scattering corn on cultivated land might seem to be a very simple business. Where wheat or oats fall on fertile ground and there is moisture to nourish its germination, corn will grow. The Bible emphasized this throughout the Old Testament and in the parable of the sower. The God of the Jews promised a yield of tenfold and the harvest field of Boaz was a wonderland of heavy-headed corn gathered by faithful servants, and gleaned by Ruth and Naomi. The Bible contributed not a little to the mystical image of the sower, and the church took in a little of the pagan doctrine when corn dollies were brought to the harvest festival, but practical men knew what a sower really had. It was something a little more than just any man could cultivate. The sower could sow grain with his left and right hand, evenly, tirelessly for all the hours of a bright spring day, and all the days that followed, until a field was seeded and finally harrowed and rolled.

It was important to sow neither too thickly nor too thinly. To sow too thickly was wasteful of seed. To sow too thinly was not only wasteful of the labour of cultivation, but produced a smaller yield from the land. Corn was hoarded. It was used sparingly. The economy of the countries of Europe depended largely on the manipulation of the price of wheat. Bread was the staple diet of the poor. Henry VI of England was compelled to take steps to control prices in the corn markets and following his somewhat inadequate measures to regulate the sale of corn there were Corn Laws of one sort or another for more than five hundred years—without the problem being solved on the vast acreages of American, Canadian, or Russian wheatfields and this even in the age of plant pathology and effective pesticides!

The sower's place in the rural community was always something special. He ranked among those respected for particular gifts or talents as did the horse doctor, the bone-setter, the charmer of warts and the weavers of spells, the exorcist and the witch. There was a simple, physical explanation of the sower's talent. He was a man of exactly the right proportions. In modern times we often analyse talent and study physical characteristics to enable us to say why a particular runner, shot-putter, high-jumper or swimmer excels his rivals and takes the highest award at the Olympics. The sower's body articulation made him what he was. He had hands of the right size for his arm length and his stride. He walked like a soldier. Every pace on level ground was exactly the same length. He co-ordinated his arm movements with those of his legs. He picked up a handful of grain that was exactly the same every time he did so. He cast it with the same force in exactly the same arc to cover the same distance. If an aspiring sower was not capable of attaining this co-ordination he would never make his name. He would never be allowed to sow corn for his master and he would stand no chance of being acclaimed a sower! The work of the sower imposed itself on the pattern of cultivation, and the measurement of agricultural land, and a day's work for man and horses, because a sower broadcast two handfuls of grain a little over five yards, approximately two and a half to the right and two and a half to the left. The pole measurement, which before the days of metrication every schoolboy recited as one rod, pole or perch, endorses this fact. A pole is five and a half yards.

There was never a physical operation that the inventor didn't strive to delegate to a machine however, and as far back as 1730 a gentleman named Jethro Tull set to work to make the sower redundant by designing a seed drill. He must have gone back to the drawing board rather a lot for despite his best efforts the sower marched on for another two hundred years. This is not to say that the seed drill hadn't been made as near perfect as could be by the beginning of the present century, but corn has always been a precious seed. Farmers have never liked to think of wasting either seed or labour. The hand sower still stood in the background like a ghost. A step towards remedying the lack of skill, the scarcity of men with exactly the right physical characteristics was the design of the fiddle. The fiddle was an archimedian device, a spindle rotated by a thong and a bow. This turned a vane and scattered corn from the base of a hopper or chute. The fiddle sowed not only corn but grass seed. Unlike the musical instrument it could be played by anyone with enough strength to carry a couple of buckets of corn. The grain fell evenly. It was cast as far as the operator needed simply by the force of his elbow—the number of beats to the bar he played as he strode along! Neither the seed drill nor the fiddle shook the old farmer's faith in the hand sower. When the church blessed the fields in spring they blessed the sower, just as they blessed the reaper when it came to the harvest festival.

The seed drill was a horse-drawn device consisting of a long box with two compartments. One held the grain which filtered through to the second compartment where it was 'ladled' on by a series of cup wheels to funnel into spouts which allowed it to trickle on to the earth beneath. Ahead of each of these spouts was a small coulter like a finger which made a tiny furrow in the earth to receive the trickle of grain. There was a set of rollers to firm the land afterwards but the beauty of the drill was that it sowed the corn in parallel rows. This enabled the farmer to use a horse-drawn hoe. The seed drill moved at the pace of the horse, of course, but everything else did, ploughing and reaping and carrying-in. While the drill was useful for sowing corn and some root crops it was not the farmer's choice for everything. There was nothing better than the fiddle for sowing mixtures of grass. It was as necessary to return a field to grass as it was to turn the lea to sow wheat or oats. The most skilled of corn sowers was taxed by the problem of sowing grass and prob-

ably had been since the Romans brought lucerne to Britain. A handful of grass to the right and a handful to the left even on a windy
day would have been far too thick. To sow corn by hand, the sower
wore a large canvas basket hung from his shoulders like the old-
time pedlar's tray. The basket was refilled on his way up and down
the rig by one or two men stationed there to keep him going. The
sower was the most important man in the field and he expected to
be served, just as the farmer watching him expected him to sow
evenly uphill and down by regulating his pace. But grass seed was
lighter. The sower might sow grass without help but he had to have
the ability to scatter the fine seed evenly if not with two hands, with
one. Only an exceptional sower could achieve rhythm and take a
pinch of grass seed with either hand, but when he did this he didn't
move his whole arm to sow as he did sowing corn. When corn was
seeded the operation required that at a stride the left hand took a
handful of grain and was swung back low, behind the left thigh—
straight-armed. The right hand took a similar handful of grain. As
the right arm was straightened and swung stiffly back behind the
right thigh the left arm swung upwards to a point directly above
the sower's eye-level and in front of his head. Grain was scattered
by a gradual opening of the hand. This spread the corn to the right.
The left hand then returned to the canvas basket to gather another
handful. The right hand followed through in the same way. The
essential thing was rhythmic movement, a soldier-like march with
head up, looking to the front for this ensured an even spread. With
grass, which was so much finer and lighter, a right-and-left-hand
sower moved his forearms only, casting a mere pinch of grass
seed from between the finger and thumb of his hand. When he had
mixed grass to sow, with seeds of larger size, he might vary the
amount picked up by using two fingers and a thumb or three
fingers and a thumb of either hand, but there were not many
men who could do this with both hands. Indeed, there were
not many men who were as good at sowing grass as they were
at sowing corn. The rotation of crops notwithstanding, sowers
had far less opportunity to practise grass sowing. This applied
to other grains too, however. Corn sowers generally sowed
more oats or wheat, with barley second, and always far less rye.
The fiddle was the answer to sowing grass seed, and the mixtures

of corn and grass sown when land was left fallow for a year or two.

Where have all the sowers gone, one might ask? Where have all the horse ploughmen gone? Where has the corncrake gone, and the mower who cut round the nest? The mower followed the sower as the seasons follow one another, echelons of mowers with a steady stride and a whetstone in every hip pocket, a bottle in the cool grass of the hedgeside and no thought of tomorrow! As the sower had come walking, upright like a giant, the mower had come bowing and lunging, his blade singing through the tall wheat, the nodding barley, the stiff rushes sown by no man's hand but needed to thatch the rick or the roof of his cottage. Here and there a few harvesters used the reaping hook. Hay and harvest took for ever. In rain-plagued northern and western parts of the country a lot of hay would lie wasted, bleached and mouldy on the shorn field. Stooks of hand-tied sheaves would begin to grow at the ears or become rooted to the ground by a green aftergrowth from the furrow beneath the stubbles. Waste was part of the toll that a man working the land had to be prepared to pay. The priest would soberly tell him this was his lot, but a tithe was a tithe of course, a tithe of plenty or a tithe of poverty. God always blessed the bishops with a tithe of the tenfold he had promised the sower. No one questioned this, particularly the tenants of squire and church.

Sowers sowed and the mowers mowed until the middle of the nineteenth century when the industrial revolution made it necessary to improve the methods of harvesting, if not of ploughing. The horse-drawn hay reaper (there had been many attempts to produce harvesting machines in earlier centuries) was the result of much thought. It was designed to cut faster than any team of mowers could mow, to get the hay or corn down while the sun was still there to dry it with the aid of a gentle breeze. Mowers were able to exchange one form of backache for another. They walked behind the hay reaper, drawing up rows, turning the hay and bringing it into small ricks or quoils (in some places called coils) in which it weathered until it was carted to the rickyard. Mowers made redundant by the corn reaper, a similar machine to the hay-reaper but with a slower 'stroke' (because corn is never grown as thickly as grass) found themselves 'lifting and tying' instead of mowing. The machine could generally manage a whole field except where there were boulders or knolls. Here the mower would be called on to cut round the obstruction, and of course he still had the honour of the first cut. A 'road' for the machine had to be opened with the scythe before the harvest proper could begin for a lot of good corn would have been trampled by horses or dragged out by the roots as the machine passed over it. The hay reaper simply snicked down standing grass, cleanly and neatly, letting it slide over the knives and fall to the ground. The knives, triangular in shape with blades of approximately two and half inches ground on two sides of the triangle, were riveted to a knife bar. Power was provided by the large landwheel. The blades of the knife bar passed between cast iron 'fingers' parting the stalks or corn or grass as they came against them. The action imparted by the driving rod was reciprocating and rapid, as it had to be. The corn reaper was a somewhat different proposition. Corn could not be let fall over the knifebar as had been the case with the very early models, for the work of gathering it and then tying it into sheaves would have been wasteful and cancelled out all advantages of dispensing with men with scythes. Even the scythe piled the corn at the end of its stroke so that it could be easily lifted. The improved corn reaper was fitted with a 'delivery board' which could be raised or lowered by the man whose job it was to sit on the machine laying the cut wheat or oats against the board until enough had been accumulated to make a sizeable sheaf. Lifting his foot from the tilting bar or pedal, the operator allowed the board to fall back and swept the accumulated corn from it. The moment this was done he depressed the pedal once again, gathering a new sheaf. The corn reaper required two men to manage it, but soon it was fitted with a rotating flail which swept the corn over the knifebar and on to the board now controlled by the driver. The first step had been taken towards what would ultimately be called a combine harvester, but there was a long way to go to get rid of lifters and tyers of sheaves, to modify the new reaper and make it a reaper and binder.

The beauty of the reaping machine was that it employed the team used in ploughing. A well-matched pair of horses made it go merrily along. There was a difference in the yoke, however. A team ploughing was yoked to the swingle-trees of the plough but the reaper was hauled on a pole yoke like the old ox wagon. The long pole bolted to the iron frame of the reaper was rounded at the fore-end. Here there was a wooden bar a little over three feet long and linked to the pole in such a way that it moved freely when its extremities were attached to the collars of the team by straps. The main weight of the machine was taken by the long pole. The drag was the same sort of heavy burden as the team had when ploughing. There was the same swingle-tree linkage from the machine through chains and backband to the hames of the horses' collars. The reaper was a dangerous implement until it was fitted with the chain-driven rotating flail which was like a windmill. Should the team take fright, perhaps when a brood of pheasants rose under their noses or a hare sprang up, the man operating the foot bar was seated directly above the knives. He could easily fall among them. Accidents in the harvest field were often gory and maimed the victim.

A corn binder was only a step or two away however and the inventors were busy on the problems it presented. They needed a mechanism that would tie a knot in a piece of sisal twine without the fibres of the twine sticking in it and making the tying of a single knot ultimately more labour consuming than the old way of using a few strands of wheat or oats to make a band for a sheaf. There was another problem too. When the binder tied sheaves and cut its way round the field it could not be held up by sheaves already delivered. These had to be tossed to one side which meant that instead of corn passing on over the knifebar to be rolled up and made into a sheaf and dumped behind, it had to be moved across the line of advance and passed to the right. There would only be one man on the machine which would employ three or more horses. The horses couldn't be allowed to trample over sheaves which would then be ruined under the large landwheel or the knife board. All of these problems were solved. The binder had its teething troubles. The knotter would stick and sheaves would tumble out untied. The conveyor-belt carrying corn up into the gathering mechanism consisted of a set of canvas sheets laced on rollers. When these sheets got wet with dew or rain they tightened and split. Corn couldn't be cut wet for a wet sheaf would never dry out in time to be built into a rick.

The farmer who invested in the new machine had to learn where he could use it and how it had to be adjusted on different sorts of terrain. He also had to be a little bit of a mechanic or have a smith close at hand to make the adjustments needed. There had been few occasions on which the horseman had to work with more than two horses but now he had to control three and even five when the machine was needed to climb a steep hill and cut corn at the same time. Horses that had become accustomed to pulling a reaper weren't too troublesome when yoked in the large and cumbersome corn binder, but if one of the team took off or reared the man who held the reins was on a great monster rushing away at top speed. If the draw pole broke the binder bucked and the traces snapped the swingle-trees loose. When such disasters happened old men shook their heads and said they had known all along that new-fangled, complicated machinery had no place in a harvest field!

There was some truth in the criticism that what went well on the prairies of America and Canada wasn't ideal for the farmlands of Yorkshire, Devon or North Britain. The makers of the new binder depended on reports from those who went in for the machine to modify their designs. The corn binder had come to stay and the mower with the scythe was redundant. The now obsolete flail reaper was on its way to become a museum piece. Perhaps the most significant thing about this step forward was an economic change. In the days of cutting corn with the scythe all a man needed was physical assistance. If he hadn't a large family he needed helpers of one sort or another he could call on in times of need, to weed his rows, to cut his hay, to bring the corn in or to lift potatoes. Now for the first time the farmer really needed capital. He had to invest in machinery. Although he might begrudge the outlay and have to borrow the money (farmers became great borrowers of money from this day out, always trusting in the harvest!) there was no help for it. In time everything would save on labour, the agents for such implements explained.

The binder had been made possible by the invention of the knotter, which was a nice little bit of engineering in the shape of a polished hook that took the twine and looped, tightened and cut it in a few seconds while the binder's gathering mechanism held back the next sheaf waiting to be tied. The knotter was the sort of thing a skilled gunsmith might have worked on. It was certainly the most sophisticated device built into an agricultural implement until this time. It wasn't the last, of course. The great millstone of the agricultural revolution had started to turn. It would roll faster and faster and farmers would have to borrow more and more money to equip themselves for the race! A man who lagged behind and tried to save money by using less up-to-date equipment would certainly fail for he wouldn't be able to compete. The man who had six horses put two binders into the field and was always able to cut his corn when it was ripe. If he was lucky he carted it long before the wet weather came. He still had the problem of building it all into his rickyard of course and had to wait for the machine to thresh it out when the contractor finally got round to him.

The carting-in of corn was as big an enterprise as cutting it. At the rickyard the butts or corn staddles were made ready sometimes in the lag between cultivation and hay or corn harvest or on unsuitable days when a drizzle of rain prevented hay being turned or corn cut. A corn rick, something hardly seen anywhere in the best arable parts of Britain today, was a work of art in itself. It had to be symmetrical. It was almost always round, tapering outwards as it rose from the staddle to a height of perhaps fifteen feet or more according to the diameter at the base, and then rising to a cone which was roped to keep the thatch in place. A common thatch was the round rush which weathered well and shed water for the length of time the rick was likely to be standing awaiting threshing out. The rope network holding down the thatch would be weighted with stones or ventilated bricks. Only rarely were ricks or stacks covered with a tarpaulin, although tarps were sometimes used to keep the water out of the long 'sow' stacks built when the threshing machine coped with a number of corn ricks.

Before the sheaves came to the rickyard they stood in stooks, heads together, one propping another, in groups of four or six so that the wind could blow through them and keep them dry. The corn was cut when it was on the point of ripeness, and not after it had ripened if this could be avoided, for ripe corn could fall from the sheaf as it was tossed out by the binder. There would have been a loss even the gleaners of old couldn't have made good. Inevitably, in the day of the workhorse, corn was sometimes cut a little green or a little over-ripe because of the vagaries of the long season which, in the south might begin in late July and in the north continue on into October. The binder made short work of cutting the corn. All that remained was to stook it, but sometimes rainstorms made it necessary for a farmer to send his men out again to break up the stooks. They would topple the sheaves in order to expose them to the sun once more, or even to move them all to prevent the after-growth fixing them to the ground where they would rot as the grass grew into them. The aim was always to get the harvest in. This was done with carts or wagons which would traverse the field so that one man could build the load and two or three others fork the sheaves as he did so. A cart was equipped with rails to support the towering building of sheaves. The sheaves would be carefully laid in the 'box' of the cart and the builder would rise with the building, laying sheaves head and tail along the rails, one row on top of another. He would keep a critical eye on what he was doing so that the overhang was even and there was no danger of his load slipping. Even when it was roped down and on its way to the rickyard it was possible for a badly-built load to develop a lurch out of true. Occasionally wagons or carts, passing along a slope or rolling through a depression on the field, would overturn. When this happened it wasn't the danger of the horse or horses being smothered that made the carter rush to remedy matters but the prospect of a fatality if the horse was 'hung' in its collar. With the weight of its body slumped against the ground the unfortunate horse would be left with its neck trapped. If the lie of the land was such that its head was hung it strangulated. The remedy was to cut the hames strap on the collar and release the unfortunate animal. A trapped horse would usually struggle and kick wildly when it found itself hung. The carter had to be nimble and quick about what he was doing or risk injury to himself and perhaps the death of his horse.

At the rickyard the unroped cart often queued to be unloaded as a rick or ricks were built. The man who brought the load sometimes helped fork it to the builder of the rick but often took charge of an empty wagon to return to the field and build another load. The rick-builder had little time to stand and stare! If he got a spare minute he would jump down from his rick and go round its circumference, beating the butts of sheaves until they looked even. It took skill and a good eye to build a rick that when completed looked as though it could have been constructed in brick or stone because it was solid, absolutely even in its conical rise, and a delight to every-one who looked at it. Good rick-builders were almost as highly thought of as good ploughmen and their friends could often recog-nize their work. The final touch was to thatch what had been built and see to the roping. Roping was accomplished by men on four rick ladders passing coils of sisal rope to one another as the thatch was tightly tied down by the network they constructed in the pro-cess. When all was done the rickyard would be a memorial to good husbandry and the product of a year's hard work, but the ricks would soon be demolished. They were needed either to feed stock and provide bedding for animals or were threshed out to be ground into flour at the mill.

If harvesting had by this time been mechanized, so had threshing. There had been a day when all threshing was done with a flail, a hinged wooden tool consisting of a bar and a handle, the two being joined together in such a way that when the handle was swung down the bar could be used to beat the ears from wheat or oats without crushing grain. The flail was used on the granary floor but its place was taken by a horse-drawn, walk mill. This machine threshed corn a great deal easier than it could be done by hand. Into the bargain it winnowed the chaff off and tumbled the straw through a chute into a strawshed. The horse operating the mill walked a circle, pull-ing a bar which, by means of a crownwheel and pinion, turned the machine, generally inside the barn. The steam threshing machine applied the same principle, substituting an engine for the poor old horse. Those who had no horse walk-mill relied on the steam thresh-ing machine. Although the machine was powerful enough the farmer was still expected to provide a large team of helpers to serve it. Threshing day was a major event in the farming year. Neighbours came to help. The kitchen worked overtime providing food for the contractor's men and all those who came to lend a hand. Even cart-ing water to keep steam up was a tiresome chore. A corn rick would as often as not have its colony of rats and have to be surrounded by a wire fence into which dogs and indomitable small boys, armed with sticks, would be dropped to kill the vermin; but all round them the work went on, smoke billowed, steam jets hissed steam, belts slapped and chaff blew in the wind from morning until night. Now and then the farmer himself would stop forking or supervising and thrust a hand into the corn spilling from a chute into a sack to sample his grain. He calculated his return not from counting ricks but from the way a rick 'threshed out' and the quality of the wheat, barley or oats he held in his palm. There was no more reliable method. The man who did it had waited perhaps eight to ten months for the result. His ploughmen were generally helping with the threshing and wondering if he would give them a shilling for beer at the end of it all. Threshing was always thirsty work and it had a certain finality about it that nothing else in the farming year quite equalled. At the same time there was no more satisfying experience than immersing a hand in that torrent of threshed corn.

4

The Beast of Burden

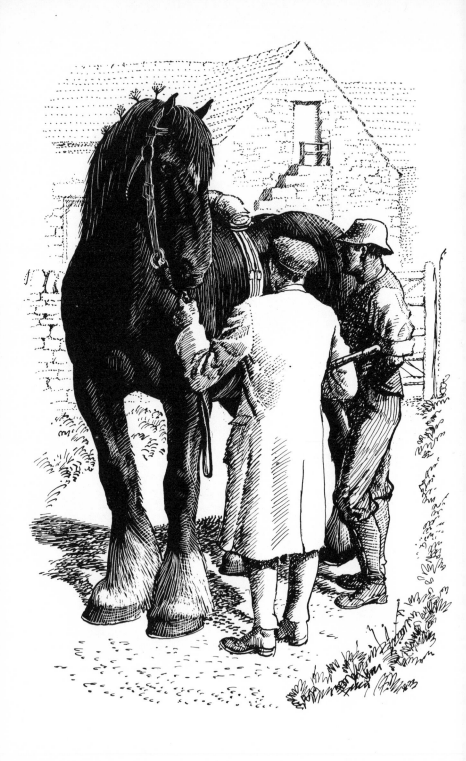

I T HAS always been the nature of man to turn to something else to carry his burden. Who could blame our forefathers for putting their burden on the ass, the camel, the ox and finally, the working horse? Man may have been promised three score years and ten but most of these promises were made to relieve his mind—and persuade him that there was a heaven where he would ultimately receive his due reward! In fact men died with little over two score years behind them. Even with the ass to carry the load the peasant barely scraped a living cultivating his olive tree, his vine or the corn he sowed, cut and winnowed after he had threshed it on a sheet. It may have been the increasing weight man put on the back of the docile ass that made the mule so obstinate when one beast was crossed with another, but the ox was more powerful than any horse even the Romans had, and it was an uncomplaining, bovine beast. An ox would walk steadily from the toe of Italy to the Alps pulling a wagon or a plough. It did this across the plain of Lombardy. It would do it from one horizon to the other and while the population of the various countries that employed the beast was small, by virtue of wars for possession of fertile ground and the hazards of everyday existence, this pace was satisfactory enough. The ox may have hauled supplies but it wasn't an animal really suitable for war. All the most successful warrior races had cavalry. They came on horseback with sabres and lances as fast as their horses could bring them. Their heavy brigades, their knights and sturdy yeomen at arms, rode on heavy chargers. The more robust these horses, the more devastating the charge. It was the breeding and development of this heavy horse of war, a deep-chested, stout-bodied, strong-boned charger that ultimately led to the breeding of the heavy workhorse. Most men who lived at the latter end of the age of the heavy workhorse gave little thought to the history of the beast. They probably imagined that it had been there for a thousand years. The Romans had brought horses through Gaul. Barbarian armies had swarmed into Europe from the east on horses as wild as themselves but all this was remote from the great Shires, Clydesdales, Suffolks and Percherons that were the background to the world of farming in the eighteenth, nineteenth and early twentieth centuries. The proper history of the heavy workhorse is closer to two hundred and fifty than five hundred years. The 'generation' of the working horse went side by side with changes in the nature of peasant farming and the needs of a growing urban population. In an incongruous way the heavy horse might be seen to have been part of the industrial revolution. While man with a mechanical bent struggled to invent machines to weave faster and to burn carbon in crucibles to improve the smelting of iron or to produce steel, the horseman created horsepower in the stables, an animal with the strength of more than a dozen men and almost as heavy as the ox because it was the descendant of the great horse of war. Doing this the horse-breeder crossed one animal with another until he had the shoulders, the legs, the powerful back and all the other characteristics he looked for in an animal that would haul great loads not only across stubble plains and hay-scented meadows but up the steepest hills and through the deepest mire. He grew to love this animal when he worked with it as he loved no other creature except perhaps his wife and his dog. Unlike a great many people now concerned with horses beyond the day of the working horse as we knew it until the 1930's, the agricultural horseman was not a sentimentalist. There was little room in the old horseman's world for anything but practicality. The bond between the horseman and his team was mutual suffering in wind and ill weather when they struggled across rain-soaked fields on those grim winter days with even bleaker twilights.

The principal agricultural horse of England came to be a magnificent animal called the Shire, a horse the townsman might have been forgiven for regarding as no more than an out-sized animal God put on earth to pull the brewer's dray or bring sacks of flour from mill to bakery. The Shire was a draught horse but an animal with a history going back to what was known as the English Great Horse or the Black Horse. The Black Horse in turn went back to the Romans on one branch of his ancestry and on another to the Flemish horse, weighing more than a ton and standing no less than seventeen hands high. This Flemish horse is said to have come from a large-footed, hairy-legged horse, a subspecies of the wild horse of the steppes found in the forest areas of central Europe. Time has played havoc with the genetic lines of man and horse and there is no reliable record of the heavy wild horse with dinner-plate-sized feet in anything turned up by archaeologists or anthropologists. It was certainly the great Flemish horse that provided the bone structure of the Black Horse and the Shire. A Belgian horse's sloping shoulders did something to produce the Clydesdale from the Shire perhaps but the Shire was the older breed, and heavier than the Clydesdale. Black Shires predominated, as perhaps might have been expected, but breeding produced brown and bay Shires and the same colours in the Clydesdale. The Shire was the most popular breed throughout southern and western England. The Clydesdale, as its name suggests, was a northern favourite. The horse of East Anglia was the Suffolk. Each breed was favoured for particular work on particular land. The breeders of the Suffolk horse admired its finer legs and its massive body. They claimed, not without reason, that it was an indomitable puller of loads and rarely jibbed where lesser breeds gave up. The Shire put his great shoulders into the collar and dragged the haywain out of the badly rutted meadow. His large feet at least gave him a great grip of the ground but his heavily 'feathered' legs mired and got very wet. This made the northern horseman favour the cleaner-legged, less massive Clydesdale, an agile, mettlesome animal, tall in the leg and with a finer head set upon an arched neck. The man who bred Shires would never admit that the Clydesdale was an improvement on his animal. The man who favoured the northern horse condemned the Shire as a slower-witted beast, heavy in the leg, strong in the back, weak in the mind. Less of stature and yet a wonderfully resilient, staying-power beast, was the Percheron, a horse that was of French origin, taking its name from an old French district known as La Perche. La Perche was part of the departments of Orne, Eure et Loir and Sarther. Here they had bred

an animal owing its blood strain to the famous horse of Flanders
and the more highly-strung Arab. This mixture of blood fined down
the large Flemish animal, and made it leaner and lighter and the
perfect horse for the stage coach, which, until the construction of
the railway network, was the only means of transport across most
of England. The Percherons were in the main grey in colour
although blacks and bays were bred. There was never a Dickensian
Christmas card artist who wasn't inspired by a vision of grey stage-
coach horses! Man bred for colour as well as bone and stamina,
but the Suffolk horse, perhaps due to a certain conservatism in the
people of eastern England, was a chestnut.

There were, and still are, a number of other breeds of horses that
might be included as beasts of burden. All of the heavy breeds are
still extant and jealously nurtured by societies dedicated to their
preservation, but harness horses and trotters, once mainly utilitarian
animals, are in a special category. They were cherished as stable animals for broughams and gigs. Hackneys served to draw coaches of
one sort or another. The fast mail had been made possible by relay-
ing teams of hackneys until the railways came into their own. After
this the hackneys served on as heavy hunters, as the country doctor's
beast, the rector's mount, the squire's favourite. At the turn of the
last century farmers who possessed good trotting horses vied with
one another racing along country roads to or from market. There
was nothing quite so exciting as the sight and sound of a fine trotting
horse on his mettle and going like the wind with harness accoutre-
ments jingling and his mane flowing. The trot is a particularly
attractive gait in which, as the right foreleg is lifted the left hind
foot moves simultaneously, as opposed to the gait of a pacer in which
feet on the same side move together. There is a military precision
about the movement of a pacer and a Folies Bergère flamboyance
about the high-stepping of a perfect trotter. Both gaits are the result
of training. Some animals, like some breeds of gundog, achieve the
movement and rhythm almost without effort. Others have to be
curbed and checked and schooled until they are perfect. The trot,
while more spectacular, is a little slower than the speed achieved
by a pacer. Grand though the gallop may seem when depicted by
painters of hunt or steeplechase, it loses its attractiveness when the
horse is pulling a gig! The gig seems designed for the trained horse,

for the perfectly turned-out horseman with burnished brass and shining leather. This is something every townsman should see, at least once in a lifetime, in order to understand what the horse meant to man and continues to mean to some people right on into an age of diesel fumes and lead additives that poison the air.

While the squires and the hunting gentlemen bred hackneys and fine-boned hunters, farmers who ploughed more than one team, and some who kept as many as thirty heavy working horses, often bred their own. A brood mare would be excused labour and kept in comparative luxury for her labour pains. She would be an animal with a good pedigree and her foals highly-prized as replacements for the stable, although they might, if they were particularly good specimens, be shown and sold to the highest bidder. The brood mare was served by a travelling stud horse who had a circuit like that of a tooth-puller or the old-time ballad singer. The stud was advertised in advance and bookings taken before the stallion set out on his tour. He was walked round the countryside and presented himself, or was presented by his groom, immaculately turned out. Only rarely was the animal blinkered but generally leather haltered. Massive though he might be, and both Shires and Clydesdale stallions were sometimes all of eighteen hands high, he carried nothing and wore little but a backband fitted with pouches to accommodate curry comb and dandy brush. His forelock would be braided and perhaps his mane too, and his tail would be knotted artistically, his nails oiled. His heavy road shoes flashed in the sun. Even the tallest groom, and for some reason all grooms were of small stature, was dwarfed as he hung at the halter when this great beast pawed the road snorting as he waited to meet the chosen mare or to be stabled for the night. The outcome of these nuptials would in the course of time be the arrival of a gangling foal to be critically appraised before its future was decided upon. Whether it was a gelding or a filly it would have to be broken, first to chains and then to shafts. This was a business for the expert horse-breaker. Few farmers who knew the psychological makeup of a yearling trusted themselves to break it in. The hallmark of the breaker was left on the animal for the rest of its life. There were various approaches to the business of breaking a young workhorse which had more to learn that the hackney or trotting horse. It was introduced to the sort of work it would have to do by first being loaded both in chain yoke and cart harness. A well-broken horse was advertised as 'broken to chains and shafts' and often, in the early days of the motor car, the advertisement included the information that the animal was 'steady in passing not only the motor car but the steam threshing machine'. The business of breaking was exciting and sometimes fraught with danger. The young horse would rarely have been shod, for shoeing was an ordeal faced later, but could deal a lethal blow with its powerful hindfeet or rear and toss a man like a kitten's plaything. Once the young horse had been cajoled into accepting the halter it was no great job to get it to submit to the bridle. To this the breaker would attach a long rein and sometimes made double sure of restraint by fastening the end of the rope to a ring-stake driven into the ground. This allowed the young horse movement in a circle. By one means or another it was made to trot round and round and finally slowed, sometimes by sheer fatigue, to a more or less steady walk. It was not a business at which the horse-breaker welcomed an audience, because it was not for the squeamish. A binder whip might be used rather freely. Horses are infected by human fear or nervousness and the ultimate aim of the breaker was to subdue the beast. He wasn't called a breaker for nothing! Some horse-breakers insisted that a horse's spirit must be broken before or it would never be amenable to discipline. Not every horseman agreed with this of course and not every horse-breaker was brutal and heavy-handed. Nevertheless, in the early stages of its breaking-in the young horse might show the whites of his eyes and lay his ears on his skull rather often. He would snort as horses always do when excited. The sweat would break on his flanks and foam on his mouth.

Once sufficiently 'gentled' the horse could be stood to be collared and another milestone passed. The collar was a large and heavy piece of saddlery which, because of its shape, had to be inverted, slipped along the horse's head and then turned round again to slide down and rest on the animal's shoulder. Some horses would always be inclined to toss the collar if this stage of breaking-in was mismanaged but once this was successfully over, the collar could be fitted with hames and chains so that the load could be attached. A large log or railway sleeper would do at first but a swingle-tree

either of wood or iron was advisable to keep draught chains clear
of the restless animal's feet. When the swingle-tree was hitched up˙
there was always much to-ing and fro-ing to make the final link with
the billet of timber. The breaker controlled the horse with long reins
draped over the horns of the hames while his assistant led the horse
forward. Nothing could be completely accomplished in one session.
The lathered horse might have to be unhitched when it was on the
verge of taking off and no longer listened to pleas or curses. There
would always be another day and a quieter mood. The essential
thing was to avoid leaving an unpleasant memory likely to make
the second attempt as futile as the first, for this was really the opposite of training a horse to become amenable to command. Persisted
in it might result in serious injury either to the horse or the horseman
who took it into the field to perform its allotted task.

Once training in chains was accomplished the next step was to
break the animal to shafts and load-bearing under a heavy cart
saddle. Here again methods varied. With some horses there had to
be a very gradual accustoming to the cart saddle. The weight of
this tightly-stuffed bit of saddlery was as much as a young horse
could tolerate. The heavy leather saddle had a deep iron channel
across it to accommodate the cart chain. The leather from which
the saddle was made was thicker than that of the heaviest boot or
of most heavy leather armchairs. To get the young horse used to
weight on his back trial might first be made with a sack stuffed with
straw or filled with bran or oats. After this the breaker or his assistant
might hang across the animal's back and talk to it as it bore the
weight. Men who strapped on a saddle had to be careful that the
horse didn't lunge forward or kick; but when this was done the next
thing was to get the breeching in place, locating it under the tail of
the horse, with chains dangling ready for hitching to the shafts when
these were lowered as the horse was backed into the cart. In order
to get the horse this far the bridle would almost certainly be replaced
by one fitted with blinkers, or blinders as they were called in some
parts of the country. Blinders prevented the horse from seeing too
much to the side or rear, although this restriction of field of view
sometimes tended to make the animal even more nervous. A critical
moment was when the back-chain was down in the saddle channel,
for if the restive horse decided to go as the horsemen struggled to

complete the linkage of chains between hames and cart and breeching, another crisis might arise and the whole thing have to be gone through on another occasion. There was never a young horse that didn't have tantrums when its breaking seemed to go well. Even the well-broken draught horse, born of a long line of firstclass working horses, didn't take kindly to fetters and chains particularly when they seemed to have become a symbol of toil—the yoking of a cart, the hitching to the plough, or some other implement chosen for the day.

A farm horse might work most of his life without walking on a hard road. Some horses were infrequently shod but others needed the attention of the smith at least once in twelve weeks and more often if they had a lot of road work—hauling corn to the mill or coals from the nearest railway station. There were problems in shoeing a young gelding for in addition to the ordeal of having his feet pared and trimmed and generally made ready for the shoe, there was the fire, the heat of the hot shoe and the roar of the hearth when the smith's assistant worked the bellows. This was something a working horse became accustomed to, but for the young horse it was more unnerving than a child's first visit to the dentist. In an atmosphere of burning nail, coal dust and grit, to say nothing of acrid smoke, it was no wonder a young horse trembled and quivered as the smith ran his hand over its withers and down a foreleg to lift a foot. Sometimes the wretched horse would be hauled tight to a ring in the wall with more than one man on the other end of a long rope to keep it close tied. The shoeing smith had to have considerable courage for horses vary in temper and temperament as much as human beings. Where one may be reasonably calm another will only submit when brought to its knees. What the first shoesmith accomplishes or bungles other smiths inherit. The terror in having shoes clamped red-hot to his feet, and nails hammered close to the very quick may stay with a horse for the rest of its life. The present-day shoeing smith recognizes his failures and will often comment on the failures of others when he has trouble with a pony. With the generation of working horses it was the same. Such-and-such a horse would be dubbed ill-tempered because So-and-so had put its first set of shoes on its feet. Every craftsman, good, bad or indifferent, signed his work whether he was aware of the fact or not, just as every parent puts his mark on the child he brings up—and perhaps more hotly disowns his black sheep on that account. What made a young mare or gelding a good horse was something more than its careful breaking-in or shoeing. It was the stable in which it was housed, the stablemates alongside which it worked, for with all horses there is a great need of companionship. Horses take to one another or they don't, just as they take to their masters or resist them. With the right team-mate a young horse also needed the right horseman aware of his likes and dislikes, who would feed him and water him in a way to which he would be accustomed. This attention was most important. An experienced horseman always learned the abilities of individual horses. One would never work at a particular task but excel and plod on at another, while his neighbour loved a certain kind of work but never gave of his best at something different. A horse that could be lured with a ladle of oats or called in without a bribe could often be relied on to bring stablemates off the pasture. There might however be a cunning horse who would grab the oats in greedy mouthfuls and kick the ladle out of the horseman's hand, showering him with clods of earth thrown up by his heels as he galloped off. Every horseman appreciated that there was such a thing as a horse with a perverse sense of humour, just as there were mean horses, crafty and downright untrustworthy ones. A horse that disliked a carter might jam him between his flank and the boards of the stall or might even run the wheel of the cart over his foot! A playful horse would take a delight in leaving a man with his coat flapping, rendered buttonless in a minute by expert biting-off of each button from top to bottom of the garment. A small boy who got under such a horse's feet might be caught and held by the hair. A mean ration of oats might lead to the stableman being held prisoner when the aggrieved horse put one of his own great feet on that of the unfortunate man. Horses that were workshy were no less skilful in avoiding labour than some of the men who were supposed to work with them and put a shoulder to the wheel. Lazy horses (and ill-tempered ones) found their way to the sale ring however, just as lazy carters and horsemen found themselves at the hiring fair.

For all their labours the horse team received a small reward, three or four hours' feeding in a working day, a bed of straw in a warm stable, a gallop on the pasture on a Sunday. The 'input' would be a few bushels of oats and a bran mash or two. The 'output' was something no one really appreciated perhaps until the poor old working horse, like the horseman himself, was made redundant. The horse worked his lifetime and was a very, very old animal if he ever approached forty years. More often than not he went to the knacker in his mid-twenties. A matronly mare past her prime, might fetch twenty pounds if she could pull a cart at harvest, but the long-toothed, hollow-backed nag could hardly expect to be pensioned. Foreigners ate horsemeat (a lot of our own people did too, had they but known it) and the knacker came quickly when he was asked to put an animal down. The horse coper sometimes bought the toil-worn workhorse and doctored him up for the innocent to buy, feeding him, it was said, with mash liberally charged with lead shot to fill out his belly, filing his long yellow teeth, giving him a tonic to brighten his eyes and even caning his hollowing back to make it swell a little. Such devices never fooled the man who really knew horses. A dealer might insist upon trotting an old mare up and down while he held her bridle in a way that made her move to hide foot faults or an inflamed shoulder, but the purchaser of an elderly horse expected that and ran his hand over the beast to feel for galls, pressed here and there and stood back and waited until the aged beast was allowed to relax and shift her weight from one foot to the other. If the modern car-dealer is the world's favourite image of a villain he has surely inherited the horse-dealer's reputation. The man buying a second-hand car generally knows the market into which he has ventured and the farmer needing a horse was always on his guard against the perfidious dealer.

Bringing a young horse into his stable or buying an old one to serve some special purpose, the owner of these animals had to invest in suitable harness. The necks of horses, like the necks of men, vary in size and in the case of a working horse the collar had to fit well. Blinkers, bridles and other strap harness might be adjusted a notch or two. The collar had to fit snugly and the saddler's great talent was collar-stuffing, a business very few saddlers can turn their hand to in these times. A horse of fifteen or sixteen hands would have a neck and shoulders in reasonable proportion to its height (the hand measurement is a hand's breadth and not length of course, and arises from the simplicity of using hands and feet, one for horizontal and the other for vertical measurement). At a pinch a suitable collar could be found on the peg in the harness room or the stable, but a young horse would fill out and grow thickset and needed to have his collar saddler-made, fitted and adjusted by a man who could tell by feel exactly where to fill and where to relieve the padding of the collar. A fastidious farmer would have no truck with second-hand harness or hand-me-downs but the poor man, of course, had no option and a poor man's horse wore ill-fitting gear. Nevertheless, like pouring a quart into a pint pot, the man who tried to put a small collar on an eighteen-hand gelding discovered that its head wouldn't go through the aperture or, if it did, the collar rested far above the animal's shoulders. Since a working horse could only per-form, whether in chains or shafts, by bringing its shoulders and the full power of its body into the collar, there was no way in which a large horse could wear a small one's collar.

Every task a horse performed brought home to the horseman the need to keep it well nourished and looked after. The countryside was generally well-supplied not only with saddlers, harness makers and blacksmiths, but with old-fashioned horse doctors and vets. A condition powder for the working horse was advertised in the 1880's as being 'strongly recommended for producing a beautiful smooth skin, for bringing horses into good condition, giving tone to the sto-mach, increasing the appetite, purifying the blood!' It was also a remedy for treating 'grease' and swelled legs, a tablespoonful being given twice a week in the mash and the horse doing its work as usual. The work always depended upon the health of the animal for this was the real age of 'horsepower' which, incidentally, was the proper name of the walk mill—the horsepowered threshing machine. Horses pulled box harrows as well as ploughs, chain harrows, zig-zag harrows, land rollers, turnip and carrot-sowing machines, Tull's seed drill, as well as rakes and hoes, reapers, binders and every kind of wagon in its turn. The makers of engines to replace the most versatile of animals struggled to sell a so called donkey engine for the same money as that paid for the horse. The man concerned with physics and pure mechanics sat down and worked out a formula based on raising 33,000 pounds one foot in one minute. In some rather obscure way this was derived from the power of the horse although the theorist was quick to concede that this was notional. A horse was a horse, was a horse, and no one could say with certainty what a good horse might or might not do. It hauled dismantled engines up mountains to help with the building of dams. It carried the spoil from mines. It performed prodigious feats when teamed up with dozens of others. It had hauled the nation from the slow pace of the oxen of earlier days into the faster-moving world of the eighteenth, nineteenth and finally the twentieth century. It blessed the survivors of the hungry forties and pulled binders. It brought everything briskly into the world of horsepower and pounded along the Strand and past the Bank of England carrying beer barrels or passengers on horsebuses. It reminded everyone at the drawing-board that the world was bound to go faster and faster. Ultimately the working horse would be put to grass, immortalized by the great artists such as Constable. It would be recognized as part of the nation's history by very few, even the oldest blacksmith shoeing show animals or delicate racehorses. Was there ever a secret horse-man's word? The mystics might believe that there was. For the young farmer of the 1970's the most puzzling thing would be how his grandfather had managed at all depending on horses, facing not so much the long hot summers of yesterday, but the inevi-table wet ones when pure horsepower was never enough!

5

The Herdsman's World

EVOLUTION, to which Darwin drew attention, to the great consternation of those who preached the Genesis theory, wasn't enough for the man who kept cattle, even before dairy-farming became general. The production of beef depended on the breed of animal a particular climate would support and man didn't dare to wait for such a slow process to work itself out. He was himself involved in evolution and he either survived or died by doing things or leaving them undone when he had learned a particular lesson. Today there are herd books and pedigrees even some of those who claim Norman ancestry might admire, but beyond the records, cattle, like men, go almost all the way back to the garden of Eden. The nomads brought stock with them but there were also wild herds, animals with characteristics necessary for survival in less hospitable country. These improved the strain. Everywhere time and circumstances combined to ultimately produce such breeds as the shaggy Highlander, the Aberdeen Angus, the Galloway, the Ayrshire, the Welsh Black, the Devon, the Hereford, the Shorthorn, Lincoln Red and dozens more with beef and bone or milk yield, including the queens of butterfat originating in the Channel Islands. This is much-condensed history. Whole books are written about individual breeds of cattle. Many more will follow, for man will never have done, even if he fills his milking parlour with three-thousand-gallon cows artifically inseminated from fuming nitrogen cold-storage banks of semen straws, and immunized against every known disease! The herdsman has already come a long way. He had a long way to come and everything he did depended upon communications. There was a catalyst in the nineteenth century—the railway system, the network of communication which began to take shape after 1830. The railways meant that the product of pasture-land farming could be conveyed to towns and cities before it 'went off'. Before the railway, communication was largely by roads inherited from would-be conquerors and those old droving ways along which cattle meandered from north to south or from west to east—to prosperous areas where the money was. The roast beef of old England came on foot, losing weight between grazings, resting a while to recover on the outskirts of places like Smithfield. A cattle truck wasn't the first inspiration of the designer of a train. Railway wagons carried beaver-hatted bankers and affluent merchants until the novelty wore off and shareholders began to look for a larger dividend from the movement of coal and iron or timber and tallow. The milk train was soon building in the smoke of shunting yards. It would become almost as important as the first-class sleeper to the grouse moors and it would run every day, God blessing men like Brunel and the importation of navvies from Ireland.

It is wrong however to give the impression that towns were without a milk supply until Stephenson came up with his Rocket. The cry of Milk-oh was one of the oldest cries of London. Almost every growing city had on its outskirts (or even embraced and isolated), farms that provided the citizenry with milk. The milk might be blue from much watering and would horrify the modern medical officer could he take samples of it, but it did a little to provide calcium and curb rickets in the slums. Milk, however, killed or infected almost as many people as it nourished in a day when it was sold by dipper measure from a can the milkmaid carried. There was no refrigeration. Mr Pasteur had done his best to convince the world that milk could be almost as lethal as a bomb unless it was treated. The legislators still had to get round to standards of hygiene when authority enforced other regulations about adulteration and butter-fat content.

The farmer with more milk than he could get to the town when his unpedigreed tuberculin cows were excelling themselves, could feed his excess to pigs or turn to the production of butter and cheese. There were drawbacks to diversified dairy farming. It was simple enough to produce milk and not unprofitable by the standards of the day to sell it in the town. To 'process' it meant investing more

time and labour in the business and there still remained the market-
ing of the butter and cheese. In the case of cheese-making, which
depended on the rich grassland of dairying country, a man needed
to install a vat or vats, control the temperature of the main operation,
have a source of hot water and steam and a dairy large enough, or
with a specially fitted loft, in which cheese could be stored first in
the press and then on the shelf until the cheese matured.

We have time-honoured names for English cheeses—Cheshire
and Stilton—there are so many famous cheeses now that it would
be hard to list them all, but the sad truth is that our English cheese
was not very highly thought of before organized dairy farming
became well established. Cheese was made by most farmers' wives
when there was an excess of milk or cream, but this domestic enterprise was no more than that, a woman's world of frugal duty like
making butter and keeping a few hens. It was no wonder that con-
noisseurs of cheese drooled over the cheeses of France, Switzerland,
Italy, Holland and the rest of Europe. People in these countries had
studied the business of making fine cheeses with the same attention
they had given to producing vintage wines. Peasant cheese-making
was confined to the family and flavouring a cheese with herbs
or seeds or wine was something the British preoccupation with
organizing things could never encompass. When we really began
to produce good cheese it came from the farm properly equipped—
a sort of factory. What became famous as English farm cheese was
quickly taken up by industry in the mid-nineteenth century when
the first cheese manufactories were set up. Anyone who has ever
cut himself a slice of real farm cheese can understand the old dairy
farmer's contempt for factory products! There never was a better
cheese than the one set to mature in the cheese loft, a hard-crusted
cheese with muslin embedded in its skin, a cheese that never turned
mouldy overnight (nor did the bread of that day!) but was as mouth-
watering a week later as on the day it was first cut. There is a wealth
of nostalgia in the thought of that cheese, the bread, beer and pickled
onions of grandfather's day!

Farm cheese was not an all-the-year-round production for a
number of reasons. One of these was the fluctuating output of milk.
Another was the maintenance of the right temperature in a large
and generally cold and draughty dairy at different times of the year.

Everyone knows that milk will curdle in hot weather, but for cheese-making it has to curdle under control. Curds are the raw material of cheese whatever its colour or flavour, and curds are made by using rennet. In the early days of dairy farming some cheese-makers would actually manufacture their rennet. Rennet is obtained by processing the stomach membrane of an unweaned calf. There are other ways of making it from particular plants, but the calf was the first selection of the man who discovered how to make curds. Added to milk, rennet quickly separates the fat from the thin watery liquid now called whey. The manufacture of farm cheese entailed the raking of the curds formed in the vat and breaking them up until the curdling was quite complete. The curd would then be rolled to force out all the remaining liquid and finally milled or shredded before it was almost emulsified again as it was pressed in a cheese press. The cheese press was rather like the smaller brewery barrel with a spring-compressed lid. Some presses did their work by having the lid forced down by means of a turned wooden screw similar, on a small scale, to the wooden screw used by book-binders. Once the cheese had set it would be tipped out of the mould and stored in an airy room until it was ready for market. Samples of a batch might be taken with an auger but cheeses which ultimately fetched up in the better class groceries would have the same mummified appearance as the perfectly preserved ham in its muslin jacket. There was, of course, something complementary in the production of these items. There had to be. The dairy farmer who made cheese had nightmares at the thought of so much liquid waste and nearly always kept a herd of pigs to which he fed the whey by-product. It was often a case of swings and roundabouts, even in ordinary milk production, for on hot days milk would go off when it had been through the cooler and the separator, but pigs wouldn't turn up their noses at either whey or sour milk so readily as people of the towns.

Few farms ever produced large quantities of butter because butter-making results in buttermilk, a nourishing drink when it is fresh or processed to make it keep, but not the best of milk products to keep in a dairy in the bad old days. Farm butter was generally made in two different sorts of butter churn. One was the 'end-over-end' churn, a barrel spun by means of a handle, the inside of the barrel having vanes or slats against which the cream would dash as the churn was turned. The carefully prepared cream was poured into the barrel churn and a sealing lid screwed up firmly. The dairymaid or dairyman churned at a steady forty revolutions a minute for as long as it took for the glass to 'break'. This was when a small inspection 'window'—no bigger than a modern tenpenny piece—ceased to look coated with milk and presented a mottled appearance as globules of fat began to combine. A venting valve would have to be pressed every so often to release the gas generated by the separation of butterfat from liquid. At a point when large lumps of yellow butter might be seen on the inspection window the churn would be opened, water poured in to further increase the consolidation of butterfat, and the churning resumed. Finally all the liquid would be filtered off and the brined butter tipped or scooped out on to a tray or board. The other sort of churn revolved horizontally and was sometimes equipped with a central spindle fitted with propeller-like blades to facilitate the churning of the milk. It, too, had a sealing lid and a venting valve but it took more turning. It was usually designed to handle a larger quantity of cream. Once the butter was removed from the churn it had to be 'worked' up with butterpats which a skilled dairymaid could do with fascinating efficiency before she put up her packages, using moulds to make the pats more attractive. Great quantities of buttermilk would be drunk by farmworkers on hot days. It was esteemed for increasing a man's virility and would be as much in demand as a pint of best ale.

Butter is churned at a temperature of 56°F to 58° in summer and 60° in winter. In a factory, cream for buttermaking is ripened artificially by using a culture of lactic acid bacillus but in the old days of farm butter—it was almost always a well-salted product to ensure its keeping—and before the cream separator, milk would be set out in pans for a day or two, creamed, and the cream kept without being allowed to sour. The skimmed milk would be fed to pigs or calves already feeding at the trough. Brining the churn was always an important part of the operation of farm butter-making. The buttermilk was filtered off through muslin to prevent the loss of even the smallest nuggets of butter. In the rich dairy country of the west of England milk was also creamed for making their famous Devonshire clotted cream. There was really no great mystery attached to the product. Clotted cream can be manufactured anywhere. Making it is, in fact, no more than 'scalding' the cream after milk has stood for about twelve hours. This is done by lifting the pan onto a stove, keeping it there until the cream on top of the milk 'blisters' and then removing it so that the scalded cream can be skimmed off and put into jars or cartons. Like butter-making, the making of clotted cream was never more than a sideline of organized dairy-farming. Factories could produce good cheese and butter more economically by handling the by-products of buttermilk, skimmed milk and whey in other processes. The herdsman and even the dairyman, cared very little what happened to the milk. Both were interested in the animal producing it, the faithful, cudding cow.

Even when at last there was a milk train and a more flourishing market for milk, the dairy farmer who increased his herd still had to rely on hands to milk. The strange thing about the milking cow is that she responds to an individual. She is a creature of mood and particular character. Any experienced herdsman will endorse this. The dairymaid who milked the cow held the secret of the milk yield quite literally in her hand. A cow gives milk in response to the suck-ing of her calf. Perhaps not even the modern milking apparatus de-pending on the pulsator can do as much, but the skilled hand-milker was worth more than the few shillings a week she received for attending on the milking cow in her hour of need, early morning and late afternoon. A badly milked cow is never in the best of health. Contented cows, as the large dairy combines began to tell the world in the twentieth century, give the best milk. Snuggled in at the side of the heavy-uddered cow to which she would croon a song, the dairymaid first milked and finally stripped the cow dry, carried her uncovered pail of milk up the shippon walk and tipped its contents into a churn that might or might not have a covering. The udder of the cow was rarely washed. Sometimes the teats of a cow sup-purated and the farmer insisted on the milk being included in the bulk trundled off to be sold. Doctors and vets cried out in protest. Medical men all along the line looked hard at milk and the sicknesses it imparted in its untreated state, but beggars couldn't be choosers and a cow giving milk was too valuable a beast to be left to the knacker. Disease might cause havoc among dairymen, herdsmen and even people who had never seen a tuberculin cow before they died; but at this time when the binder was trundling into the corn-field, the internal combustion engine making its first flatulent noises, and people holding out their bare arms for vaccination, inventors were working on the milking machine. This was a suction device which they hoped would dispense with the pretty singing milkmaid. They were not very successful, however. A calf is not a suction in-strument! Its tongue and mouth coax milk from the cow's udder. Old farmers were well aware of the difference between an everyday milker and the one they chose to milk their cow at a show. There was a world of difference between the new machine and the hand-milker. Only wealthy dairy farmers with large herds could afford to toy with the new machine. The drudgery of milking would con-tinue until a machine was perfected and the unit became as indivi-dual as man could make it. It took quite a time. Side by side with its development scientists, vets and forward-looking dairy farmers with the money to go in for it, looked at the possibilities of tubercu-lin-tested cattle, tuberculin-free cows. This was a matter of public health. Sadly no one gave as much attention to a serious complaint in cattle and another scourge in man, brucellosis or contagious abor-tion, a disease not as devastating as foot-and-mouth, but over the years almost as serious a scourge because it persisted. Diseases in cattle all too frequently also affect those who work with them. Just as the miller or the man working in the grain store suffers from lung trouble and may contract an incurable condition known as farmer's lung, the milkmaid might be infected with cowpox. This in a strange way held the secret of vaccination, for it was noticed that milkmaids rarely had the disfigurement left by smallpox and in fact cowpox was to some extent a means of immunizing. Since cowpox was not always mild and benign—if it didn't disfigure permanently it could mean protracted suffering for the person infected—a clinical approach had to be made. Vaccination was the outcome. Some people who had had cowpox (the writer among them) were so heavily charged with the vaccine that doctors considered vaccina-tion in such cases a formality. Foot-and-mouth, until it came under special regulation requiring the destruction of an entire herd of cattle, the unaffected along with the obviously affected, was dealt with in the old days simply by constructing a sort of funeral pyre and burning the diseased cow or cows. This wouldn't guarantee there would be no fresh outbreaks from the original source but the old farmers often succeeded in subduing the plague or keeping it as well hidden as the squire did his mentally deficient relative! Abortion was, and still is, a business involving carelessness when a cow calves and the placenta or afterbirth, sometimes called the 'cleanings', were thrown on a midden or a dead-at-birth calf was left lying and not buried or destroyed in one way or another.

It was the comparative poverty of dairy farming that built in the drawbacks to public health and the health of herds, particularly small herds of little more than twenty milking cows. A man producing milk on this scale might have to make a decision to put down a cow that represented five per cent of his capital investment. It was a lot of money. If he had to pour his milk away he was in despair. He was even in a tight corner if he had to milk his herd himself. He had a lot to do in the day, not only delivering his milk, perhaps to a retailer in the town or to one of the new co-operative creameries (processions of milk carts and horse-drawn drays would queue at creameries in days before motor transport became the rule) but he had to scald and sterilize his churns and other equipment with boiling water and have everything ready for the next milking. In summer the difficulty was to keep things cool. In winter it was no longer a business of milking and turning the cows out, but of feeding them and cleaning the shippon as well as working in the dairy. A milker would rise at five o'clock and work at milking for perhaps two hours or more. The dairyman worked steadily on. The herdsman worked all day in winter, foddering, feeding or preparing the food for his standing-in cows. A milker needs an exact and well-balanced ration of food because a cow is not simply an animal into which hay is stuffed at one end to produce milk and manure at the other. Protein and minerals are as important to the cow as they are to a nursing mother. In the old days, however, things were done by rule of thumb or what grandfather and great-grandfather had held sacred. A cow might be given molasses, hay and diced turnip in no carefully measured or worked-out quantity. A cow that gave a lot of milk was prized until she went dry. It was thought that she owed her ability to make gallons of milk to her blood line rather than her diet. This was largely true, but the man who began to weigh food before he put it into the trough and learned that all milk is not just grass deserved his reward, although for years he would have to argue over a farthing a gallon while listening to experts on nutrition telling the world how important milk-production really was. Farming of any description was never going to be easy and dairy-farming would always have more downs than ups it must have seemed to the herdsman concerned with breeding the perfect milking cow.

The answer to the problems of milk distribution, milk production and the survival of those engaged in it seemed to be solved by what was called the Pool. Milk had become the raw material of a developing food industry. Chemists devoted their time to the discovery of processes by which it might be converted into substitutes for a variety of materials, and milk bars sold milkshakes and cakes adorned with ersatz cream—cream had suddenly become too precious to put in tea or coffee! It was, after all, the butterfat and milk that contained as much as 3·5 per cent of butterfat was highly esteemed. At that figure it passed the creamery and Ministry of Agriculture's minimum standard. The layman might wonder how this test could apply when cream rises naturally to the top of the milk; but of course milk, even at the source of supply, is not only cooled but is handled in such a way that actually ensures the distribution of butterfat through the bulk of the milk. This continues when milk is poured or pumped and the butterfat test is a simple one. On the other side of things, while there is a danger of milk being watered, by the same test the ratio of milk to water is obvious.

The lowing herd still wound o'er the lea, to be milked by hand well into the present century when, all at once, even the man with two milking cows and a source of power, a small generator or an electricity line, was able to equip himself with a milking machine. The lowing of the herd became less significant than the purring of the engine providing power for the pulsators of the machine. Vets came along with everything needed to cope with milk fever, mastitis and all the ailments to which cows are heir. One result of this careful medication with antibiotics before the cow calved deprived the dairyman or the farmer's family of an oldtime treat—'beastings', or custard made from the first lactation of a cow with a new-born calf. Beastings were richer and thicker than even the Devon man's clotted cream but not to everyone's taste on that account. They were of a much richer shade of cream than everyday cream. This first food for the young calf certainly called for a very special sort of stomach membrane. It was rich indeed and was squeezed from the cow almost like squeezing sausage meat from a sausage. Old people swore by beastings as nutritious food. They had a mystical faith in such things and would give beastings custard to an ill-nourished and perhaps rickety child. Whether or not it was really good for a child no one ever seemed to dispute. Perhaps it was. On the other hand it may have contained some of the organisms present-day believers in antibiotics strive to eliminate. People either liked beastings custard or were revolted by it. Those who liked it would often feed untreated milk (still warm from the cow) to their offspring and who is to say they didn't in a roundabout way immunize their children against a great many ailments, even if occasionally they must have made them rather sick and wan for a time?

While some farmers managed their herds personally, those with large acreages of pastureland and accommodation for large numbers of milking cows often took a herdsman or dairyman into their service on a profit-sharing basis—long before anyone in manufacturing industry had considered such Utopian dreams. The herdsman would then have a great incentive to look after his master's stock, to look closely at animals when they were sick or when they were calving or coming into season for breeding. In some cases the herdsman would be allowed to run his own herd within the herd. This kind of thing had long been the practice, although on a very small and modest scale, with arable farmers. A man planting carrots or potatoes planted so many rows for himself along with those for his boss. In the matter of dairying this practice still continues where in arable farming it has probably dried out. The herdsman's job was not only to be nursemaid to the herd, to feed the calves that were weaned, but to finish them out for market (if they were bull calves) or consider them as possible replacements for cows gone barren and sold off for slaughter. The herd books took account of pedigree bulls but the great drawback to the breeding of better milking cows was the prevalence of breeding bulls used, not because they were particularly good animals, but simply because they were bulls. It would have been better if many of these had been slaughtered. The inheritance of tuberculin cattle was bad enough without its being perpetuated by diseased sires.

As soon as tuberculin-testing began there was a problem in keeping the higher caste animal away from inferiors. Testing was long drawn out and expensive and the security of farms had to be reinforced with double fencing. The price of a tested herd was heavy because until every negative had been settled and the whole herd pronounced clear the market was no more attractive than it had been. In the early days tested milk would be hurried away, not in the old-fashioned churn but by tanker, to feed sickly children and hospital patients. It was regarded as a very precious commodity by doctors and hospital physicians, although it would soon be taken for granted by the general public who would probably never know the trials of the herdsman instructed by his master to have the herd tested and 'go T.T.'. A cow, a horseman would often say, is not the cleanest of animals and has always been prone to more ailments than the horse. This is quite true, but the cow has been more used and abused than any other domesticated beast. It has been underfed and illfed, bloated and starved, poisoned and neglected throughout the greater part of its life with the peasant. In the past hundred years it has received the attention it deserves as a main producer. The horse produced only horsepower. No one really preferred horsemeat to beef, except the perfidious foreigner, despite the horseman's cry that the horse was clean. He had been taught this even in the Sunday school while listening to accounts of tithes paid to kings and beasts fit for sacrifice but not for roasting. The pattern of agriculture throughout almost all of Britain always involved the cow in one way or another. Although there are what might be called granary counties, most parts of Britain encompass mixed farms, arable farming and dairy or stock-rearing farms on which crops are, and were, grown to support the production of milk or beef. There may be sheep in the meadows but sheep the peasant had long ago decided were for the uplands, the Downs, the hills of Wales, the moors of the north. This was so in the wild country beyond the Clyde, at least until cattle invaded and drove the sheep back and their owners out and across the ocean. The circle was then finally complete. The cattle raiders who had gone south for beef were finally displaced by drovers and herdsmen!

Fashions in beef cattle and milk-producing cows change in decades rather than generations of man. Invasions from the Continent have brought us Holstein and Friesian and many more. The expert breeder of the British beef animal improves what he gets or discards it for something else in a few years. There was a time, shortly after the Ayrshire cow was acclaimed as the tuberculin-tested wonder, when the milk of Friesians was scorned as a kind of blue water with skimmed milk added, but men and cows change and the Ayrshire is not quite what it was or seemed. The once de-spised Friesian has come into its own but no one wants to know the blue-grey Holstein. The deep-chested, typical English Hereford bull, a superb beast, has no way of knowing that the fickle herdsman is dallying with French beef and scientists are cutting and weighing steaks, measuring protein input and protein product to the detri-ment of a sometime favourite, or to please some passing fancy, were the truth but known!

6

Hodge in the Nineteenth Century

A T THE DAWN of the nineteenth century whatever inspiration rippled through the brain of inventive man, Hodge the labourer was concerned with survival, as his father before him had been. It was a matter of feeding hungry mouths, the Hungry Forties were yet to come of course, along with all the inventions for the improvement of life. Mr Telford and Mr McAdam would vie with one another in methods of road construction—while turnpikes held a stranglehold on free passage from one place to another and tollhouses barred the way. In this century the steam engine would be a wonder, but at first not a great deal faster than the stage from London to Edinburgh (which took fourteen days) until someone discovered an easy way to roll steel for track-laying. When this happened the railway reached out to far-away places and burrowed through mountains to get there.

Hodge lived in squalor in a cottage in the village entirely owned by the squire, in a stable loft, even among the cows and pigs. If he had some small degree of skill and was a good man with cattle or a man able to plough, he had a farm cottage. The word tied probably was not used because there was no other sort of cottage. A landowner was an owner of property which he might rent. He was also in absolute authority and the man whose face didn't please him had nowhere to go. Pleasing the master meant engaging female children to work as kitchen maids, the male ones to work in the master's garden or to scare birds. It meant the mother of the family being on hand to help out in any way required and her husband also being at the beck and call of his master, without work when it rained, and labouring all the hours of daylight when needed to earn that

shilling or so he paid in rent. There was, of course, a happier side
to living under patronage. In very hard times her ladyship or the
rector would have soup to dispense or discarded clothes to distri-
bute. Charity was a great virtue and its patrons would call in a miserable itinerant to hew wood or clean a cesspit, not for a sixpence,
but for a workhouse token, a local coinage entitling those who
sweated to a bed and perhaps a plate of skilly. This was provided
at the 'institution' which would not be given that name until the
word workhouse was associated with such acute misery at the hands
of the notorious workhouse master.

There was a great drawback to the idyllic life in the remote
country, served not by McAdam's fine aggregate, rolled and consolidated road clad in asphalt, but generally by winding muddy lane
or potholed track. Hodge would never be able to do as the industrial
worker would—organize himself for collective bargaining. He was
trapped out there and isolated. He was in fact the cheapest machine
the farmer could have wished for. He didn't need a lot of fuel. When
he broke down he recovered by a natural process. When he became
obsolete he went to the workhouse. In the meantime he bred replacements for he went to bed to save the candle. It was the way
of the world to bring children into it and to thank God for them,
even although they died in infancy or before they saw their teens.
The problem of a too large family lasted only for as long as it took
for a hard life to settle the fate of the unfit. The fit soon grew old
enough to hoe a row, glean a stubble, gather faggots or hold a pony.
Hodge, the father of the family, suffered a number of occupational
diseases from lack of a balanced diet. When he worked closely with
cattle he might suffer from tuberculosis, but the incidence of this
scourge of the lower classes was greater in the industrial parts of
Britain than among the rural population. Hodge's lot was rheumatism, broken down, and specifically defined under several headings
from rheumatic fever at about the age of seven, to muscular rheumatism in his middle years and 'chronic' in his old age. He didn't die
of rheumatism. He died because he wore out. He wore out fighting
his natural inheritance, but his children died of a variety of plagues
entered on parish records and sometimes on their gravestones. At
six months, among the angels, poor little Nan died of fever, typhoid
or scarlet? What did it matter when so many more were being

entered on the record in the same week, the same month and almost every month. Rheumatic fever was more prevalent between October and spring. An eight-year-old boy who contracted it would never be transported, or even know the dame's cane for very long if he happened to attend the church school. Rickety children were as commonplace as rickety stools and sagging beds. They were congenital weaklings, it seemed, and might as easily have died of convulsions, which every baby had when it needed to be fed on whatever was available to feed the entire family. Every summer there was a culling of the unfit as flies bred up and diphtheria rasped the throats of mother and child alike, bringing them to a pitiful end because no one had the slightest idea that soil pits and the open sewer or village ditch bred the plague. In the cities medical men sawed bones in bloody aprons with no more thought of the dangers of infection than the butcher selling meat in the dusty street. The country doctor was out there to look after the health of the upper and middle classes. Hodge was said to be as strong as a horse. His cottage swarmed with children, pale-faced children maybe, hungry children who would have become far, far too numerous without the fevers and the annual plagues which carried them away. They too, when they survived, were their master's inheritance. He might not sell them when he sold the farm or the village but they had nowhere else to go.

The level of poverty among farm labourers was never labelled as 'acceptable' as unemployment is labelled today, but unemployment was really what poverty was about, so many mouths to feed, so little work available and wages so low. In autumn and through the winter a ploughman ploughed and a carter carted what crop or dung was to be carted, but the bulk of the rural population lived hand-to-mouth for a good part of the year depending upon casual employment. A ditcher could only clean a ditch when a prospective employer considered he could afford to have ditches cleaned or his landlord insisted upon hedges and ditches being attended to. A farmer had to make his rent and be there on rent day to pay it over, respectfully approaching the agent's table. His problems were Hodge's problem—how to make ends meet. Hodge did it by keeping a pig in a sty behind his cottage if he could find enough to feed it on—potato peelings, some wasted barley, acorns and bread perhaps. The man who could afford two weaners was sure of bacon from one and money from the other when he sold it. He kept half-wild fowls that scratched where they could and he ate their eggs when he located their laying-away places. He often ate the fowls themselves before the winter. In the spring and early summer his wife would be reduced to making nettle soup. Bread and dripping the children could have if the family had enough of both. Often there was dripping for favoured cottagers who begged at the kitchen of the big house, but it was sometimes only available if they had been seen in church on Sunday. The ungodly deserved to suffer. God in his mercy took their miserable children out of this world. Their parents, who wasted their substance on ale or gin (neither cost so very much more than a loaf of bread), would suffer eternal damnation.

The damned turned their hands to anything. They might not be able to feed a pig because they had no farmer from whom they could beg or steal its food, but they kept a lurcher dog and fed a ferret on bread and milk. They poached. The rabbit in their stewpot was more than a godsend, it was the reward of craft and cunning. When something better came into the net or snare it lasted no longer than the warrener's rabbit. They didn't stop to consider whether they might have had a claret or a burgundy with their pheasant or partridge! When the keepers were too watchful and there was more danger of being caught, the labourer looked in the eaves of his cottage and netted the sparrows. He went out and studied where the small birds roosted in the ivy on a wall and he netted them there. He found places where he could trap and snare birds without the keeper being at his elbow. All his captures were plucked and dressed and put in the pot. Sparrow-pie was a frequent treat after harvest and in winter, but thrushes and blackbirds, finches and every other sort of bird helped to stave off starvation. The law, of course, was on the side of the man who had inherited land, or owned it as a result of legal enterprise, and it protected him accordingly. It was not, after all, his fault that work was scarce and food to build sound bone too expensive for the casual labourer. A lean and hungry Hodge worked harder than a fat one and was more biddable, but the law had to keep an impulse to help himself under restraint. Because a bird was free to fly where it liked Hodge wasn't to be encouraged to think that it belonged to no one and no one cared for it, any more than he was to be encouraged to think that God Himself didn't care. Through the hard times of the Hungry Forties with the famine and the dismaying effects of potato blight, it became necessary to frame new laws governing poaching, to make it quite explicit what trespass was and what the rights of an owner of land were. Without such laws anarchy would have prevailed. There would have been no order in society. There certainly would have been no charity to alleviate the sufferings of the poor and Charles Dickens in his day would have been denied his most heart-moving plots. Copperfield's story would never have been written. Society would have broken down. Hodge would have died without someone to provide him with casual employment or pick him out of the line at the hiring fair. It was necessary at this time (when great craftsmen in gunsmithing like Joe Manton were designing percussion cap and finally breech-loading guns), to defend the woods and game preserves of the large estate with more than men and trip wires. This was done with mantraps and spring guns although both were made illegal before the century was out. Hodge was the first genuine poacher, the only one to deserve the name honest poacher. Indeed Hodge was even tolerated out of the pangs of conscience his landlord sometimes must have had over the poor working and living conditions afforded his less useful tenants.

The poaching laws of the nineteenth century were designed to fence Hodge out and define his offences as surely as land enclosure defined the limits of ownership. Poachers were listed as those who trespassed in pursuit of game, unlawfully entering land either by day or by night. Game itself was defined to include almost anything that walked, ran, flew or swam. In 1815 it was deemed that a man who stood outside and shot into private land would be held to have entered the land. If he sent his dog on to the land he himself had trespassed. The Night Poaching Acts made it unlawful to kill a rabbit even on the highway or take it there (or on enclosed property of course) with net, trap or snare. If the poacher were in company with several others and only one of them went into his lordship's preserves all of them were equally guilty. The rabbit belonged to the owner of the land or his tenant but this was not quite enough until the Ground Game Act was framed in 1880. Hodge's position as an idle poacher or trespasser after a rabbit with a lurcher dog was made quite clear. The Ground Game Act forbade the use of a gun to kill hares or rabbits during night time—one hour after sunset until one hour before sunrise. It was necessary for anyone found on land 'in pursuit of coneys' to produce authority in writing from the owner of that land or his agent. The penalties, apart from loss of the bag and the confiscation of whatever implements had been used in securing it, were likely to be three or six months in prison. A poor man rarely had any way of raising a fine. The repeated offence, implying a contempt for the law and an addiction to poaching, brought more harsh treatment. It also meant dispossession of the cottage the offender's family occupied. When the Hungry Forties came and the potato famine spread, penalties for offences on the estate became yet more harsh.

The potato had for a long time been as important to the labouring class as bread. Its cultivation absorbed a great many man hours per acre. Until the potato spinner came on the scene it was dug with forks throughout the potato–producing countries of Europe. It was a crop that called for more attention than swede or mangold and it was a very important item in the economy of food production until it failed in the year 1846–7. The cause of the disaster was almost as new as the steam engine. Potato blight, a parasitic fungus which the learned dubbed *phytophthora infestans* was practically unknown until 1840 but it struck like the black plague. The famine it produced killed people who had lived on the potato and who had taught the colonial American to call it the Irish potato, this despite the fact that North American Indians cultivated it before the first white man set foot on their continent. Potato blight contaminates the earth. The spores of the fungus wash into the soil. Blight turns the potato into a slimy mess and where it has struck the cultivation of that plot of earth the following year is futile. The disease struck Ireland harder than other parts of the British Isles because the people there depended on the potato. The hunger of the Hungry Forties became acute. A cynic, or someone who had always had a full belly, has found it necessary to define hunger as a gnawing sensation in the upper abdomen (some people will contest that the sensation is in any way localized) bringing on lassitude, faintness and headaches. It can, it is said, be suppressed by swallowing indigestible materials.

In the case of Ireland's famine there were plenty of indigestible materials, including Indian corn, but the suppression of hunger was temporary. The tragedy for agriculture was that potato blight was spread through diseased seed. There had been little thought given to the spead of disease by animals, let alone seed. In the nineteenth century there was much food for thought, if not for the bellies of the miserable labourer or the children working in the cotton mill. The scientist, if he knew that potato blight spread at a temperature of 70°F and in such a summer thrived like the green bay tree, hadn't communicated his findings to the peasant. The latter didn't at first notice the rusty patches, birthmarks of *phytophthora infestans*, on his precious tubers. The potato failed and agriculture in general was in the worst depression anyone living could remember. The inventor, with his head bowed over the drawing board or the glare of the steel furnace blinding him, didn't think about food. He went on inventing. The scientist went on pondering why people bitten by a rabid dog always died once the symptoms became apparent or why arsenic killed men glazing pots.

The agricultural labourer's position in the structure of society was at the bottom of the heap. He was not a freeholder or copy holder. He had no vote even when the Reform Acts were passed in 1832 for he hadn't the means to qualify. Members of Parliament were forced to show some respect for those newly qualified to elect them as a result of the reforms but Hodge hardly drew more attention than the scarecrow in the field he had cultivated. He waited for the burden of his calling to be lifted. The promoters of new inventions waited for the impoverished farmer to somehow find the means of buying the new machine. When Hodge finally did become enfranchized and qualified to elect his man to Parliament he found it wiser to support his master's man, and his master, when he happened to be a tenant farmer, generally found it wiser to support the landowner's man. In Wales tenant farmers were dispossessed for failing to do so, despite the fact that there had never been a century in which there was greater pressure for reform and secret ballot. There was no danger of Hodge, when his turn came, and he could vote in secret because of the Ballot Box Act, sending a radical to Westminster off his own bat. Hodge was over-ruled or out-voted by the community in general, long accustomed to taking at least one step back after, or before, taking two steps forward. Hodge himself, for lack of education, was a born conservative, a simple man who, if he didn't trust his master, set great store by her ladyship's smile and her good deeds, the rector's benevolent greeting and the perverted logic that what had brought the old gaffers to their ninetieth or even their ninety-fifth birthday couldn't have been bad. So long as beer was cheap and God was up there in Heaven it was no use battling against things that couldn't be altered! Hodge was laying the foundations of what the sentimentalists would call the good, the golden days of long ago, when a man was content with his lot, his bread and cheese and the air scented with new-mown hay.

The schooling of Hodge's children was a matter for the parish. The parish controlled the family, decided when they were destitute and in need of help and when the children might be released to help Farmer Giles get his crop in! The schoolmistress or schoolmaster was paid a pittance because the community was never prosperous. Even when the plight of the miserably paid and brutally exploited labourer resulted in independent boards setting the standard of agricultural wages—differing from county to county—the increase in the wages bill was reflected in the market price of farm produce. Competition from abroad was more than the British farmer could bear. It must be said that completely integrated peasant enterprise, with every member of the family working in it and taking out nothing in wages, can never be overcome by an agricultural set-up employing labour and paying a living wage. Only automated farming, as envisaged in the twentieth century, could do better than the natural commune. In the face of a paradox the British farmer of the nineteenth century had to buy what he couldn't afford and make it pay. He had in fact to make Hodge redundant, slowly and steadily over the years, without using the word, without looking him in the eye and saying it was no use, he couldn't do the job any more. In fact all this was done and said. The age of the machine was well on the way as the stage coach was replaced by the train, which would in time make even the carrier's cart a thing of the past. A day's travel was becoming something more than the distance a man could walk or even the distance his horse would carry him when he could reach the railway. It was the world a man could see that set his standards, framed his demands, gave him a conception of a new horizon. There hadn't been very much of this at second-hand in the teaching at the parish school. Young Hodge was taught enough to be able to count sheep perhaps. He was generally left illiterate but taught to show respect to his elders and betters, to take off his cap when summoned by the squire and never to get in his way. The squire was next to God and to emphasize the fact sat in a pew down at the front where he could doze through the sermon if he liked, or frown when the rector let his enthusiasm for the tenets of Christianity run away with him, forgetting to explain the spiritual meaning of the truth that man does not live by bread alone.

Hodge and his offspring had never been militants. They were in fact born conservatives. They had been forced to conserve what they had and to rely on their own efforts. They appreciated that a man who possessed anything needed to think of tomorrow and how he would manage in harder times. The squire had his problems. He hadn't been brought up able to get along on a slice of bread spread with dripping and warmed with water from the kettle, a salt herring or potatoes in their jackets. Who could expect a man used to port after dinner to drink wormwood? A man born to property had much more reason to conserve! The squire really needed to be able to count for he had rents to tally up, stock to number, wages to pay. He really loved Hodge and Hodge loved his master. Sadly for Hodge, the squire himself was doomed. The Hungry Forties were for his breed, paternalistic, benign or otherwise, the last straw on the load. Squires had been harvested from the beginning of the century, going down before the flails of reform affecting franchise and the ballot box, the employment of children, the general concern about public health and even the basic rights of man. What life and living is about is change, and what the world wanted was change, a rebellion against colonial tyranny in America, a revolution in France, an industrial one to follow—right out into the sleeping countryside.

When Hodge grew old he became a charge on the parish and since he couldn't be put down like an over-worked, hollow-backed horse, he had to be accommodated in the workhouse. Every sizeable community had its place for the impecunious, unemployable old people.

These were often endowed cottages, charity dwellings administered by a board headed by the local landowner and members of the local bench, plus the rector, the schoolmaster and the parish clerk. Merchants and others here and there with a rare and almost unique compassion for the suffering of the poor would leave provision in their wills or during their lifetime endow a charity for the poor of the parish. It was upon such Christian benevolence however harshly administered that the bearable old age of redundant or obsolete Hodge depended. What was handed out was recorded and moral judgement passed on those who applied for help by the clerk or the magistrates administering funds. A sixpence was a lot of money. A sack of coal, a few faggots of wood were a great bounty bestowed on a family shivering in a damp cottage. Poverty for the labouring class was generally a disgrace until it became unbearable and pride disappeared. The administration of charity without the grace of true charity helped underline the proper place of the lower orders. Beggars, the Victorians said, can't be choosers. Hodge had no choice. He went thankfully into the charity dwelling. He could expect the parish to bury him if he had no surviving children to take care of him, in which case he had no headstone. The parish record would testify to the fact that the clerk had paid the undertaker and the gravedigger. The rector didn't stand overlong at the grave with valedictory oration. What was there to say about a man who had been at the penny school for a few weeks before becoming a bird-scarer, a hedger, a nursemaid to a herd of pigs, had died of old age after being a charge on the parish in his declining years—not out of its debt on the day his ashes went to ashes or dust to dust?

There was always at least one means of escape for the son of the old Hodge. He could enlist in the army. The squire or his lordship was often a military man and blessed such initiative. He was often himself colonel of the local yeomanry and young Hodge, when he marched off, knew he could come back into the fold if he survived the campaign against Napoleon or whatever adversary the reigning monarch or government had turned their wrath upon. The army fed and clothed the sons of the poor which the community, the parish, largely objected to doing, or really couldn't do in any adequate fashion. The sight of the fields of the Lowlands, the meadows and the cattle of Europe were part of the education of the raw country boy who marched off and sometimes only limped a little when he came back again, improved by his vision of a new world, the value of money, the price of a man's life, and some conception of the bargain he needed to make with society in order to enjoy what was his birthright. All the while he plodded on through the nineteenth century, Hodge, however low his intelligence, however slow he had been to respond to the birch, or even the lash when he served in the navy (agitators and people often in trouble with authority were handed over to the press gang in some places to discourage the captain and his lieutenant from marching in and taking his legal quota) had been made aware of change on every side. If change hadn't put more money in his hand, more clothes on his back or more food in his belly, it was there on the farm, on the land—the easier way of cutting hay, cutting corn, digging potatoes, ploughing. A far-sighted man might have seen that the horse would go out of fashion and be replaced, that the problem of hauling the plough would be solved, that electricity would come out of the laboratory and one day bestride the cornfields and the engine take care of everything. A generation of mechanics was born. Their brilliance was being applied in everything from grinding coffee to peeling apples. Along the way the discard, the scrapheap would grow and grow as cranks and eccentrics tried and failed. Even the steam plough would be relegated to the junkyard or a museum of outsized bygones, but a lot of the principles would be retained and improved upon until they were almost perfection and the inheritors of them would shake their heads and wonder at the ingenuity of man, how he stuck so persistently at solving a problem, producing a chaff-cutter or one of the many stationary pieces of equipment with which the farm became equipped—and there were scores of them. The seventeenth and eighteenth century had been notable for the flintlock gun and such quaint and cruel machinery as dog-powered spits and churns, and the human treadmill, but the mechanic of the nineteenth had changed the principle of most old-fashioned things, looking again at the dreams of Da Vinci perhaps, and wondering all the time what could be done to make a train run faster, take the horse out of horsepower. In his small world and without being a great reader even when he had mastered the alphabet, Hodge was unaware of the imminence of major change. He lived like a peasant in the path of an invading power. The power, the irresistible object, was rolling down the slope to overtake him, to change his life and the way of life throughout the rural world of the squire, the farmer and his labourer, to change the education of his children and regularize it so that it would no longer depend on the twopence or penny paid for lessons, or the whim of the controlling body set up by church or those with property.

The tractor, which would haul everything into the high speed era to come soon after the First World War, was in the minds of those working on the petrol engine. It was a question of efficiency of design, input and output, and the way this could be geared. It was also a matter of wear and tear. A horse always responded to Hodge's spoken command when a plough or the modern binder was in danger of going end–over–end. The internal combustion engine would at first have to be coaxed into going at Hodge's accustomed pace and be made to respond to his slow physical reaction. It would take some time to educate Hodge in the mysteries not just of operating the machine but starting it when it was not in the mood, and keeping it fed and content to go on. Peasants are renowned for their wits rather than their ability to educate themselves. They are adaptable and not put off by theoretical drawbacks. Hodge whether he liked it or not, had to be taught the rudiments of a system designed to make him forsake the horse and work much faster than he had ever worked before. A bloody revolution may produce instant death. It rarely produces instant improvement in living conditions, as those who were to witness the major social revolution of the twentieth century would see, and those who instigated it, and had to deal with the peasant, would have to admit.

_____

7

The Happy Countryman

TO APPRECIATE the nature of rural life and understand why even the present-day countryman is where he is, one needs to identify a certain pattern of development in the way of life of people as a whole. The weave becomes an increasingly open one. The drift from the land is imperceptible unless in a period significantly marked by some major event, near famine, war, some new and revolutionary method of doing things. These events rarely have anything specifically to do with the way of life of the dweller in the country but affect the livelihood of a whole nation. Prosperity in an industrial area has always lured away the man whose security is subject to the elements, the growth of corn or livestock, the price these things command in the city. The fabric of life in the country was much stronger when districts were almost self-sufficient or in other words, when it was possible to eat the egg the chicken laid and feed the chicken on the corn that was harvested on the field. Even so, not even the most frugal countryman could survive by taking in his own washing. Living off the land is a fond dream that must dissolve when an implement has to be bought, grain traded for a spade or a plough. To say precisely when and why the countryman moved out of the parish and took himself to the barbican poses a chicken and egg conundrum almost to infinity; but it surely began with growing commerce between those administering law and organizing society and those growing the necessities of life. The pattern of rural life was well established and centred around the principal needs of the community when the Industrial Revolution took place. The rural population was widely distributed and the weave depended upon the fertility of land and how it could be used, either to grow corn or raise cattle or sheep. The nineteenth century and many of the events that were its milestones really took shape under the influence of men who worked to engineer steam—to drive shafts to work mills, to power pithead gear, to move trains and perform dozens of other tasks. Industry developed where these mechanical godsends were installed and used. In the country industry of a different kind, part of the whole structure of agriculture rather than with an end in itself, was located where there was a natural source of power. Even had there been a steam engine waiting to take on the task of turning the millstone when the sails of the windmill were ripped away by the gale, or a millrace was reduced to a trickle in a drought, such innovation would have unbalanced the whole economy. It would have been necessary to change the bargain between the miller and the farmer because of the cost of coal. The coal to provide steam would have had to have been hauled from the centres of distribution. The railway system couldn't make it cheaper. The windmill stood where it did and a small community grew around it, or the watermill, because here there was exchange and barter as well as a source of power. Here there was employment for women and children helping perhaps in the carding, the weaving, the dying of wool, the making of broadcloth or tweed. In another district a coach-builder used timber to build coaches, wagons and broughams. A wheelwright and a blacksmith kept him company. Their trades were complementary with those of the saddler and the harness-maker. The coaching inn gathered round it a few petty tradesmen and others who had to supplement the meagre living obtainable from doing business with the farmer and his workers. The village baker made a living tending his large stone or brick oven and selling bread to those compelled to work out of doors and unable to bake for themselves. The product of the woodland turned people into basket-makers, hurdle-makers, even coffin-makers who used elm boards. Timber also provided the material for pick-shafts and rakes (hazel and beech) and minor crafts flourished alongside the important ones that provided a wheelwright with a good living, so long as wooden wheels were needed. Less vulnerable than the wheelwright was to any change in methods of locomotion was the artificer in metal, the blacksmith who not only provided the wheel-shod, but the shoes for the horse, the hasp for the stable door, the iron gate for the mansion house and a dozen other fixtures and fittings fashioned in iron. The saddler depended on a supply of leather of course, and tanneries tended to belong in the outward sprawl of growing towns, but the hide product, when it wasn't bought for the boot and shoe industry, was quickly brought back out into the country in which it had originated to make the great heavy collar of the carthorse or the saddle of the hack his lordship rode when touring his estate to supervise his bailiff and inspect his farm tenantry. The integrity of life in rural districts was firmly established as a result of something short of rapid change. The erosion of the population in the 1800's was far less significant than in the twentieth century when, paradoxically, the dereliction of country mansions and old parsonages is less obvious than when Cobbett saw so much to deplore when he criss-crossed the southern counties of Hampshire, Gloucester, Hereford and Worcestershire. In the 1830's there was poverty as a consequence of mismanagement of funds but the crafts of the thatcher, the wheelwright, smith, coach-builder, woodman, saddler and their like were interlinked. No one was as yet redundant which, when it came to one would bring almost all of them to extinction.

McAdam's system of road-making became more favoured than Mr Telford's and McAdam or what was to be called tarmacadam, incorporating the name of its vital element with Mr McAdam's own patrimony, was changing not only the surface of the road but the amount of wear on a horse's shoes. Asphalt glazed the hills and the slightest inclines until they became as treacherous in these places as they had hitherto only been in the hardest of freezing winters. It must be admitted that the carrier's cart didn't break down in deep potholes as it had once been inclined to do. The parish or the county, having to maintain roads not under licence to the toll-gatherers, found work for the stone breaker, a man who sat out in the country-side knapping loads of stones carted to him from quarries. Road-patching kept the tarmacadamed highway in better condition and saved what passed for road transport before the day of notional horsepower from more serious competition by the newly-laid rail-way tracks and the canals. The countryman was happy enough with his lot so long as the price of corn or livestock didn't fall so low as to bankrupt his farm or leave his master in serious straits, needing mortgage money to keep his enterprise going. The happy countrymen hadn't far to go and his needs were few. This was his true wealth, a condition hardly ever appreciated by those who invariably see the countryman as so much better off than themselves. What the countryman needed was food from his plot, a pig from his sty or the opportunity to supply a service in return for these items. The cobbler didn't need shoes any more than a wheelwright needed wheels. They traded or sold their service, made a pair of wheels for a gig, a pair of shoes for a farmer's wife. There was little needed from outside the community to make this kind of transaction possible but a few nails for the shoes and a hide scraped and tanned, a metal boss for an axle and some paint for the wheels when they were fashioned. The smith needed only the iron and invested his skill at the forge, buying with the set of horseshoes he made, or the plough he fettled, flour for making bread, potatoes to go with the pork his wife pickled. The miller was a barterer too. He traded so much meal and flour with the farmer who brought grain and the baker brought him loaves when he came to buy flour. The baker made an extra penny or halfpenny by using his still hot oven to cook the Sunday dinners of the villagers. There was no need of paper money which would come in the end to replace the gold sovereign, the silver crown and florin. Tokens were really for the excisemen, the money-lenders and the clerks who neither toiled nor span.

The lifeblood of the country economy was investment of labour in raising livestock and growing crops and integrated in this was the work of the craftsman to keep wheels turning. People had to be clothed and sheep provided wool. They had to be fed and fat bullocks were taken to market. If much of the wool and a lot of the meat went to the non-productive dweller in the towns, so long as there was a market, there would be some sort of a living for the countryman. Cottage industry was diminishing as weavers took themselves off to follow their trade in the town but no one counted heads to study trends, only to gather tithe and tax. The happy countryman was still there, able to dig a potato from his plot of ground, to milk a beast he kept hobbled on the common, to have salt ham for his dinner when he killed his pig, drink beer at the inn—and dance round the maypole now that the ghost of Cromwell and the puritans had been exorcized! The ballad singer was invent-

ing folk songs to order, and old men were remembering the traditional garb and ritual of the morris dance to the mandolin. At the
fair the happy countryman, flushed with drinking strong ale, might
pay a penny for a pamphlet questioning how much it cost to feed
a standing army or the wisdom of free trade, providing of course,
he had been fortunate enough to learn to read! The world was largely
an illiterate one. It was estimated that almost five per cent of the
population were criminals of one sort or another, from footpads to
pickpockets, who haunted the fairs, the markets and the cockfight-
ing mains.

In order to curb a growing tendency to lawlessness and anarchy
in the hungry poor, magistrates were empowered to recruit county
police forces. Sir Robert Peel not only gave his name to the Peelers
but laid the foundation of the modern police force by means of acts
passed in 1839 and 1840. In 1856 it became compulsory for the authorities controlling all counties in England and Wales to provide an
'adequate' police force. This requirement was applied in Scotland
in the following year through legislation governing the policing of
shire and burgh. The Bow Street Runners began to run at Bow
Street in London. They ran on like the runaway horse, into the age
of forensic science and radar, to staff New Scotland Yard.

There was no great pace to the countryman's life in the early part
of the century. Those who had horses rode them. Those who could
afford to travel by stage or brougham did so and those without the
means travelled on foot. There was no help for it. Even when a Mr
Dennis Johnson made available the French 'hobby horse', the proto-
type of the bicycle, a most unmechanical form of transport which
a man straddled and wore out his boots to propel himself at 'something less than walking pace', the simple countryman still walked
to the fair. The first recognizable bicycle was invented by a gentleman called Kirkpatrick MacMillan of Dumfries who was also responsible for a by-product known as 'furious driving' or speeding!
The Dumfries gentleman's performance on his cranked hobby horse
encouraged a Mr Dalzell, another Scot, to eclipse what he had
achieved. The Dalzell grew into the penny-farthing. This happened
before the very eyes of the waiting public, for the old boneshaker's
wheels had been almost of a size, front and rear, the front being
just a shade larger. The penny-farthing became exactly that when

its front wheel grew in diameter from a mere 30 inches to as much as 64 inches, while its rear wheel diminished to something like a foot in diameter. This wasn't exactly the ladies' bicycle to please the Victorians for it took a degree of daring and balancing skill that might hitherto have been found in a circus performer. The penny-farthing bowled along Mr McAdam's road while Mr Dunlop worked furiously to make the solid and the 'cushion' tyre obsolete. In the meantime, with the old boneshaker (sometimes called a velocipede) already a relic, someone was working to incorporate ball bearings in the wheels of the bicycle. At the same time they changed the transmission to a geared one, with a crank wheel and chain to power the rear wheel, now matching the front wheel already reduced from something like five feet to a mere two and a half. The bicycle took the countryman who could afford it along the road at the same speed as a rider on horseback and the beauty of it was that the machine needed no feed of oats or a boy to hold it while its owner went into the alehouse. All it needed was a chain and padlock. There was no law that said it must be lit or that handsignals must be given turning left or right, but the newly appointed constable, formidably attired in his helmet and blue serge uniform, lurked to catch the 'furious' rider. He had only a few other sorts of offender to prey upon—those being drunk and riotous—except at fairs and feasts when he might gather in the pickpocket, the prostitute and the confidence trickster.

Fairs were of a number of different sorts. There were hiring fairs at which farmers and landowners engaged their servants, horsefairs at which the horse traders gathered along with tinkers and gypsies, cattle fairs at which fatstock and sheep might be sold, and what were called pleasure fairs drawing every kind of trader, pedlar, entertainer, fortune-teller and maker of sweetmeats and cheap jewellery. The fairs had their origins in history and were the landmarks in the rural year, the redletter days of the country calendar. Traditional fairs had to be regulated by law. This was attended to in the nineteenth century because it had become important to bring a degree of protection to the householder, the copyholder and the landowner. Itinerants were encouraged to move on. Some fairs and feasts had to come to an end. People living on their wits invading and remaining on common land had to be discouraged and fairs without a charter were controlled or closed down by order of the magistrates. This kind of control was really the curbing of a sort of free-for-all liberty that had marched in step with the world of gaming and cock-fighting, until cock-fighting itself was outlawed in the middle of the century. After this Hodge no longer went off openly to perch on the gravestones and watch cocks being matched in the church-yard with the parson's blessing.

Before the holding of mains was outlawed it enjoyed distin-guished patronage. The annual race meeting at the ancient city of Chester was always accompanied by a week of cock-fighting at which the birds of local landowners would compete along with those of less distinguished commoners. Fit as a fighting cock meant the very sheen of condition but once the fighting cock had been brought to this peak it was fed on bread and water, its temper shar-pened by a diet from which the more appetizing things were miss-ing. The countryman loved cock-fighting as the coalminer loved his whippet racing and the man of the potteries enjoyed watching battl-ing terriers. If he was carried away by the sport he fed fighting cocks and bred them in a pen in his back garden. The breeds were special, old English gamecocks, birds known as Lancashire Black Reds, Shawlnecks, Irish Greys, Cheshire Piles, Staffordshire Duns and many more. The rules of the sport had come down through the centuries. Cocks, said a John Ardsoif, Esq., who sought to frame them for cockpits at St James's in London in 1754 (barely a century before cock-fighting was outlawed), would meet in battle in 'faire hackle' with no leg harness. They would be thonged and hooded until matched, which would be done with spurs 'girte of the same length'. There would be one master and two holders of stakes as well as two wardens. The master would nominate his wardens and he himself would be chosen by ballot of all members. The cockpit was forbidden to ladies. It would be nine feet square. There was a penalty of twenty shillings for blinding a cock and one of forty shillings for using a prick or goad to get birds fighting. Since gaming went with cocking, and welshers were the bugbear of the betting man, there was a special punishment for the man who failed to pay his dues. The welsher would be put in a basket and 'hoist' above the pit—and remain there where all could see him, until the main was over.

Birds were set to fight one another or in a 'battle royal' which involved an unspecified number of cocks being placed in the pit and allowed to fight it out. A Welsh main involved eight birds and came to an end when only two remained. Successful fighting cocks became almost as famous as successful prize-fighters, but it was a bloody and cruel business and in 1849 it was outlawed, which didn't please the sporting countryman at all. Since he could no longer attend a legal main or enjoy his sport in the churchyard—parsons themselves often owned fighting cocks—there was nothing for it but to hold secret mains in barns or on open ground where watch could be kept in the same way as was done for prize-fighting. There was no law against breeding fighting cocks. A bush telegraph operated to tell members of the fancy where a meeting would take place. A little blood-letting, a little wager and a pint or two of strong ale were things that made life bearable. Secret mains flourished where-ever a few fanciers managed to gather, and more than a hundred years after it was proscribed by law, cock-fighting was still going on not far from Chester and probably many other cities where there had been public mains with publicly advertised meetings.

The happy countryman could never understand the squeamish-ness of his cousins half a generation domiciled in the town, and finds it hard even yet. In a day when the dandy affected extravagant refinement, the hunting man galloped wildly in pursuit of the fox and Hodge dug out the badger or went hare coursing. The words blood sport hadn't been invented. There was really no remedy for man's natural brutishness any more than there was a remedy for the pox or the clap.

There never would have been a rapid take-off into the twentieth century if man hadn't been preparing for it, however. Not all the world was dancing round the maypole, wagering everything they possessed on a turn of a wheel or a battered prize-fighter. Hodge had only a little time for recreation. Giles had hardly any either, and the new generation of gentry tended to be those who held the stakes rather than the dedicated gamblers. Mechanics, however, put their time to full use. While one school of thought worked on the possibilities of steam, another, remembering the power of gun-powder as a propellant perhaps, and certainly appreciating what an explosion within a bore could do, worked on the internal combustion engine. They were living in a time when man thought big. Most things he constructed were massive, heavy, designed to stand for ever, like the dreadnought and the never-to-wear-out, stationary steam engines being laid down in factories and mills in the new industrial areas. The first steps towards the motor car and the tractor would be unrecognizable to a man buying a sleek, Italian-styled sports car today. They were undoubtedly based on the great steam engine. No one dreamed that the engines could be lightened, scaled down and refined until they would carry a man along a road at more than a hundred miles an hour. Man had to walk before he could run, of course. The internal combustion engine was going nowhere. Like the first venture in steam it was a stationary engine. It was even turned into a sort of bastard steam engine by one inventor. It wouldn't do much for the staid Victorians who would continue to drive to church in carriage or gig and ride bicycles furiously to show off, or when they were the worse for wear. There were a few men working on the gas engine when Napoleon was doing his best to conquer the whole of Europe and Russia as well. A gas engine designed by Samuel Brown was used in a road vehicle in 1826 in fact, and in a boat the following year. A William Barnett improved the ignition of the gas engine in 1838. Men with a flair for physics and mechanics experimented with vacuum devices, worked out the compression of gas under particular conditions and tried all kinds of pistons and ignition timing mechanisms. The critics of the internal combustion engine sat back and repeated the undeniable truth that such an engine would never be as efficient as steam, but the designers of this type of engine were real engineers, practical men and simplification using flywheels to regulate the rotation of exhaust, suction and compression timing. The gas engine was far less noisy than the steam engine. As a stationary horizontal engine it needed to be cooled and it could only be employed where there was a reliable supply of fuel—town gas. Engines using heavy oil were not likely to take over from the steam engine in areas where there was no source of supply. The filling station was a long, long way off. A step towards the complete transformation of the scene was the Hornsby-Akroyd oil engine employing what was known as hot-bulb vaporization. The diesel was not so far away, and with it, the tractor running on oil. A light petrol engine was the aim of

Gottlieb Daimler whose efforts began to promise fruition when he made an engine that scaled 88 lb per horsepower in 1886. Before this engines were very much heavier. The real possibility of using them in a road vehicle was somewhat remote. High revolutions per minute and low weight were what Daimler sought, and when he achieved this he first put a motor cycle on the road and then in the following year (1887) the Daimler car. Daimler, however, wasn't gifted with second sight. He didn't see the motor car speeding off along the country road, sending up a cloud of dust and leaving the sickly smell of petrol in the air. He came down to earth in an extraordinary way and directed his attention to putting his wonderful engine into boats and launches. If Daimler seemed to be losing the way there were others who didn't. Charles Benz had fitted a tricycle with a low horse-power light engine in 1878. It didn't move the tricycle as fast as great-great grandfather could drive his penny-farthing along, but it did travel at seven miles an hour and Benz was hot on the heels of Daimler with a belt-driven four-stroke car which he exhibited at the Paris Exhibition in 1889. This was surely a most significant date for everyone in Europe, for the driver of the steam train, the ostler holding horses for his lordship, for Hodge, out there in the wilderness raking up and harrowing couch grass and listening to the birds sing.

The gas or petrol engine was certainly the most significant invention of the nineteenth century when inventiveness and mechanical research wasn't backed by wealthy institutions as it is today. It came as the crowning glory of the Victorian era, even although the Victorians were preoccupied with empire, pomp and circumstance, and mechanics stood very low in the social scale. The curiosity of man grows and flourishes like nothing else in nature. It is an extraordinary growth, as hard to predict as the mushroom springing up overnight, and as impossible to discourage as couch grass or mare's tail. Here, said the engineer of the nineteenth century, is a steam engine that will pull coals from the pit to the far end of the country, a bicycle that will carry a man who has no horse as far, and farther, than a horse may canter in a day. Here is the internal combustion engine, the tractor, the motor car, call it what you like when you need a name for the thing it will power. How could the man leading the horse know that this had happened? There were no disciples spreading the word. He could barely read. His wife and children filling buckets on the potato field, the sower walking up and down the ploughed field, worked on in ignorance, and the parson reading his sermon talked of miracles involving loaves and fishes, bread and wine, without knowing that his congregation would fade away, the wheelwright wouldn't be there to put his penny in the collection and his lordship's groom would become his chauffeur and drive him all the way across Europe instead of to and from town and up and down his tree-lined avenues.

This was all to come, and quickly by comparison with what change had meant in the early decades of the nineteenth century. The Hungry Forties were gone. Agricultural depression there might be, but mechanization was coming with a vengeance now. Kings and princes were thinking about trying the motor car, or would be persuaded to think about it almost as soon as the twentieth century began. Instead of a groom and footman the wealthy would engage a chauffeur and a man to walk ahead with a red flag, and the police would report that something would have to be done about inconsiderate drivers who forced ordinary citizens off the road, made their horses bolt, showered them with muddy water thrown up by their wheels and behaved as though they owned the public road!

Happiness is by contrast and the countryman didn't really know he was happy in his generation. Indeed, he probably longed for the improvement that would relieve him of the agony of ploughing, digging potatoes, forking a midden on to a cart or sheaves up to a rick. The nineteenth and early decades of the twentieth century would seem wonderful when the quiet road was no longer peaceful and little used, when the verges were cut back and insecticides were sprayed to kill both grass and weeds. The machine to take the agony out of the farmworker's life would be used to trim the hedges, to ravish the ditches of their cress and scented plants and leave a spoil on the bank. No one could ever accuse the farmworker of looking backwards and not looking hopefully ahead or even the most old-fashioned farmer of not buying a thing that would save him money! Politicians would legislate for road improvement, the control of every aspect of agricultural enterprise and the use of land. The good life lay ahead so far as the countryman was concerned. He had never been sure that he had had it up until now, but he remembered the 'good old days'—quite a different thing!

If the wheelwright and the blacksmith had asked what would happen to them they might have been told that they would have to adapt to the change in methods. The wheelwright would have to find some other trade. The blacksmith would have to put his mind to being some sort of a mechanic to work with the new machinery. The horseman would learn to ride a tractor. The saddler would just have to be content stuffing the collars of the dwindling number of draught horses and making pony saddles. It was going to be that kind of world now that Herr Daimler, Herr Benz and Mr Henry Ford, not to mention Mr Charles Rolls and Sir Henry Royce, were solving all the problems of the motor car and motor-mobility. No one yet put the word redundancy upon it, because redundancy was a personal thing, the fate of an individual, not a general, instantaneous disaster experienced everywhere at the same time, in a day, a week or even a year. Many things had gone out of fashion, many species of animal become extinct—dodo, bustard, sea eagle, corncrake—but the extinction of a man's way of living was not so obvious because the man didn't disappear. He didn't die. He was still there, and since what he had done for a lifetime was no longer required, he must do something else. What was happening could no more be put off than the rising of the sun.

8

The Farmer's Wife

JOHN STUART MILL's concern for the emancipation of women resulted in the publication of a work entitled *The Subjection of Women*. This book appeared in 1869 when women, especially the farmer's wife, could look forward to no more than the life their own grandmothers' had had working their fingers to the bone in the kitchen and bearing children. A Bill to give women the vote had done little to alter the facts of life when it was given no more than a first and second reading in 1870. The most considerable step forward so far as women of that time were concerned was that, if proposed and elected, they might serve on the newly-established School Boards. The proper occupation of women, urban dwellers or country girls, was domestic service. There were 123 female domestics of one sort or another, serving in big houses and hotels, for every thousand of the population of the country. These figures didn't include the unpaid domestics, those who toiled without hope of financial reward, women whose husbands and sons would have been speechless at the suggestion that they were entitled to time off and perhaps some pocket money. Life was about the family, every living and breathing member of it doing what they had to do.

Few farming households had the luxury of a 'skivvy', which was the well-meant name for a kitchen slave who performed more menial tasks. The family did its own chores, sons working for their fathers, daughters working for their mothers. Everything depended upon a willingness to accept what was an individual's duty. The woman of the house worked harder than anyone else. While she was at the baking board or the butterchurn her daughters darned, patched, mended, heated the flatiron and ironed clothes, scrubbed and polished, carried water from the well, and went on doing these things until they were allowed to get married. When a farmer's wife was confined her daughters, if they were old enough, assumed her duties. If they were not, some female relative would be recruited to run things for the short time the woman was off her feet. There wasn't a lot of fuss over childbirth among people who were involved in elemental things. Birth and death were everyday ingredients of life. The old wore themselves out and died like old dogs, crippled with rheumatism, wheezing with farmer's lung, losing their senses. The young came headfirst into the busy world, and if they weren't fed at the breast and their stomachs could stand it, drank untreated cow's milk. The child's mother might know nothing about an infant's digestive processes and still less about balanced diet, but she had the benefit of a thousand cures handed down to her by her mother, her grandmother and great-grandmother, who had cured children almost as often as they had buried them. The local witch knew all about pennyroyal if she had never heard the word ergot. She could produce a miscarriage if people accepted the fact that what was needed to take the life of an unborn infant was something as close to taking the life of its mother as might make no difference. The farmer's wife, like her sister in the town, was on a treadmill of work and child-bearing. While the townswoman brought children into the world for the owners of the cotton mills, she produced the potato pickers, the bird-scarers, the hoers of rows, the juvenile haymakers and milkers. She also fed and clothed them as best she could. She made sure that there was goose grease for rubbing on their chests, down in their pillows, herbs laid by for purging them. All of her waking hours were devoted to such things. She was the mother of a whole and closely-knit family.

In a world where there was never any shortage of unpaid work idleness was a cardinal sin. In an almost sinister way the church had long preached the virtue of labour and the need to accept the fact that man and woman had been put on earth to do no less. God-fearing people knew that it was immoral not to make do and mend. It was equally wicked to throw away anything someone else might need or something for which there might be a future use. This kind of belief supported and fortified society. Six days were for labour

and the seventh for thanking God for the six days of bondage. It
was more virtuous to prepare Sunday's meals on a Saturday. Some
farmers' wives did so. A woman who could make use of every part
of a pig but its grunt looked for no praise for being able to do so,
and got none. It was simply what was expected of a good wife. It
was, after all, no more than her mother had taught her and what
she was striving to instil into the heads of her own daughters, the
unpaid domestics working with her in the kitchen and the dairy.
There was never a time when there was nothing to do, never a season
without seasonal duties to perform. When there was an 'r' in the
month a pig was killed. When there was surfeit of eggs around Easter
the eggs were preserved in waterglass or sand. When the berries
ripened in the garden they were picked, topped and tailed and made
into jam. Daughters who were excused gleaning on the harvest field
walked the hedgerows to pick the crab apple and the bullace which
they made into jelly or wine. In autumn they picked horsemushrooms from the old pastures and made them into ketchup to flavour
the newly dug potatoes. Sometimes they made soap with lye and
mutton fat. They stood at the washtub and scrubbed shirts and the
long woollen underwear of their menfolk. They hung their linen on
the close-trimmed thorn hedge if they had no bleaching green. The
clothes they ironed, with the old flatiron fished from the fire, were
whiter than white without a detergent powder of any kind and were
scented by the unpolluted, sweet country air. All the industry of
the farm and farming depended upon these women. Without them
famine would have been real and a lot of men would have gone earlier
to their graves. If the running of a farm depended on patriarchal
influence it also depended upon a long tradition of matriarchal control from one generation to another. A man might know from his
father what field to plant and what crop to grow in it. A woman
knew how to prepare for tomorrow and tomorrow.

   The farm kitchen was the hub of the whole thing. In the early
part of the nineteenth century the only fuels available to the housewife in the country were wood and peat. The farm kitchen would
be unrecognizable as a kitchen to the woman of the twentieth century. It was a room dominated by a large open fireplace equipped
with a spit and a grill and not much else beyond a few cooking pots
and a preserving pan made of brass. The hearth might accommodate

large logs. The chimney was so wide that hailstones would sometimes roll across the floor like balls of soot. The smoke often billowed
into the room. The chimney was made large so that a side of bacon
could be hung in it to be smoked. Sometimes its stonework had provision for an oven in which bread could be baked or there was a
swinging hob to allow the making of scones above the embers of
a wood fire. Often the oven was out of doors in the yard and a great
supply of birch faggots was needed to heat the stone. In either case
the woman battled with fire and smoke and the management of a
fire was almost as important to her success as it was to the blacksmith
working in iron. To cope with all she had to do Mrs Giles rose before
cockcrow and spent the first half-hour of her working day coaxing
life into the fire once again. Once she had it lit she was off on what
was little less than a positive marathon of cookery, especially at
harvest time, or when corn was being threshed.

It began with breakfast for milkers and horsemen, the setting of
a porridge pot to boil, frying eggs in an iron frying pan along with
salt bacon and scones perhaps, but there were other things to do
between times, hens to let out, calves to feed as well as pigs. Never
for more than a minute could she or any member of the family stand
to admire the sunrise. No one dared dream of leisure. The sunrise
itself began to waste the day, climbing the sky. Leisure was for grasshoppers and the gentry who cantered across paddocks, jumping
fences for fun, or chasing a fox that could have been brought to
his proper end with a charge of shot from a muzzle-loader. There
never was a more taken-for-granted, hard-working woman than this
one, or a woman upon whom a family was more dependent. When
she had done her outside chores, and long before noon, she would
be found sitting peeling as much as half a stone of potatoes, preparing rabbits for a stew, or setting up her baking board to make bread
or scones. The family simply demolished her work. Carters and
ploughmen came hungry from the field and greedily supped the broth
she had made, drank the buttermilk, swallowed the buttered potatoes and salt beef she set before them and reached for her oatcakes
and cheese. For her there was really no tomorrow even although
she did all she could to lay up stores against it. When the invaders
went clumping back to the field or the rickyard she scrubbed her
flagged floor, scoured her heavy black iron pots and sighed for the

coming of evening, not so that she could doze by the fire or read a romance, but find time to work on her patchwork quilt or the sampler asking God to bless this house!

While the most brilliant inventors were busy inventing things to make a man's life easier they found little time to think of ways of making his wife's work less arduous. It is true that after listening to the more articulate gentlewoman they had given her a coffee grinder and a knife cleaner, both items to delight the domestics employed in the country house, but farmers' wives were not great coffee-makers and weren't looking for mere gadgets. It was the iron-founder who gave her the kitchen range, that great lump of iron to fill the big open fireplace. The range really came into its own when coal became available at distribution points handy to the rural community. The range had broad hobs. It had an oven on one side and a waterboiler on the other that might be filled from the well or the pump outside. Boiling water could be had at the turning of the brass tap although the boiler might crack and deliver a rather rusty fluid with an iron sediment. The range pleased the woman who had worked for so long with a primitive cooking fire. She stood before it like a high priestess at an altar. Regularly she had to get down on her knees before it—to burnish and polish its steels with black-lead applied with a boot-brush. If she neglected her devotions her guilt would be plain for everyone to see. The ironmongery took on a tinge of rust, almost as it cooled, because of condensation. The ashcan of the monster filled up and had to be emptied night or morning. Coalsmoke proved less fragrant than woodsmoke. Perhaps the most fortunate thing about it all was that Mrs Giles's cookery know-how needed little revision, but then the great lump of iron had no real novelty built into its firebars or oven. Old women scorned coal cookery. Younger ones took a pride in their ranges. It would always be that way. For the time being there was certainly no danger of anyone trying to turn cookery and old-fashioned housekeeping into domestic science. Everything still depended upon making the best of what was there.

The farm kitchen's furniture varied a little from one part of the country to another. Wooden settles and forms had always been popular, furniture might be of scrubbed deal or well-worn oak. The grandfather clock stood by the wall, a wallclock wagged on the wall,

an American clock became a prized timekeeper. Armchairs tended
to have horsehair stuffing that made them less comfortable to the
uncovered leg or arm. Dressers with brass handles or wooden-
knobbed cupboards and drawers were the commonest feature of the
nineteenth century farm kitchen with its flagged or tiled floor. If
the kitchen floor was subjected to so much traffic that it was never
carpeted, the parlour and bedrooms were usually covered with rugs
or carpet. In the middle of the century waxcloth or oilcloth was
invented as a floor covering. It became popular with country folk
although it didn't prove the most durable of substances even for
little-used parlours because it was made from canvas painted with
oil paint. Several coats of paint rubbed down at each application
thickened the material but oil paint never attained a very great
degree of hardness. The surface decoration would wear off, the
layers of paint become eroded. Finally the canvas of the waxcloth
would fray and wear in holes. Waxcloth may have delighted the
woman who disposed of her worn-out carpet, but it was soon out
of favour, linoleum taking its place. Lino was made from linseed
oil, flax and cork and was much harder wearing. Both linoleum and
waxcloth were the outcome of chemistry connected with the distilla-
tion of oil, the manufacture of paraffin oil and paraffin wax. Mineral
oil was beginning to come into its own. Even the tallow candle would
give place to one of paraffin wax that would smoke far less. There
had been oil lamps for thousands of years but rush candles had been
used for almost as long. The rush candle was no more than a peeled
rush immersed in household grease. Tallow dips were generally
used. They were made of clarified fat and had a flax wick. Church
candles, however, were usually made from beeswax. There was a
drawback to using beeswax for making household candles. Beeswax
cracks and shrinks when it solidifies after being melted. The tallow
dip was easier to mould and gave as good a flame, if it smoked a
little. Old-fashioned oil lamps not only smoked but gave a red flame
which was hard on the eyes and difficult to read by. Distilling paraffin brought an improved oil lamp on the scene and all at once there
was a ritual of wick trimming and lamp filling in every house that
went in for long-chimneyed brass lamps. Soon this lamp would be
improved, as gaslight in the towns was improved, by use of the
incandescent mantle, a development that probably inspired Davy's

safety lamp used in the coalmine. The brass candlestick became an ornament, as the brass oil lamp would become when electricity eventually came to light the farm. In the meantime, the tall glass lamp with its tinted glass oil reservoir and its ornamental brass stand was the pride of the Victorian housewife. Its light was reflected by the copper kettle and all the bits of brass about the kitchen and parlour, even if it was somehow more fitting to go to bed by candle-light as farming families liked to do.

The bedroom had been modernized to some extent by the busy men of Birmingham who gave the family its first iron beds to replace the sort of four-posters Elizabethans had slept in. The iron bed was trimmed and decorated with brass, solid brass knobs and rails that added to its great weight. Its great heavy iron castings made the bed almost as immovable as the four-poster until someone discovered a way of welding the frame. The iron bed, its advertisers claimed, was insect free! They didn't expand upon this. It had to be. Wood-worm had never been found in iron. Perhaps the real claim was that the bedbug didn't like the ironmongery upon which the mattress was laid. The farmer's wife who polished her warming pan and her candlesticks was pleased to find that the brass of the iron bed was lacquered and didn't need to be burnished or rubbed up. The bed was a delight to the eye at a time when ornamentation in everything was the fashion. It still needed to be made, however, and bed-making was no small task when the mattress was stuffed with feathers. It took two women to make a feather bed, but who thought of this when no one studied women's work, except to cut their pay if they happened to be working on a loom? The feather bed had to be turned, and pounded into shape once this was done. Making it was a sort of wrestling match even if it contained nothing but the down of ducks and geese. Each year, at Christmas and Michaelmas when fowl were plucked for the market, feather beds would be changed or refilled. The feathers of duck were used for pillows as well as in the mattress, but no hen feathers were ever used for these are of too coarse a fibre and have much harder quills. There was another tick-filling material used by farmers—chaff—which was stored in a chaff house below the threshing floor or the floor of the granary. A chaff bed was always much cooler to sleep in than a feather bed, and much healthier on this account. It could be changed more often and it was easier to make. The man who slept in a feather bed was always slow to rise. He slept deeply. His senses left him, and he never heard the clock chime the hour, or so his master said.

Next to the bed and her linen cupboard and blanket box, the farmer's wife set greatest store by her 'parlour'—the talking room—which might contain a fret-fronted, candle-lit piano which she or one of her daughters might play on special occasions. Almost invariably there would be a rocking chair for herself, padded footstools, and ornamental clock, religious pictures on the walls, antimacassars on the chairs to protect them from 'Macassar' hair-oil, and to go with it all, a whiff of mothballs, a slight musty smell of rising damp. Here, when a daughter was courting, her chosen suitor would be entertained, given tea from the best china, cakes from a silver cake-stand, cream from a silver creamjug if the family had such prized possessions. The strongest motive in arranging marriage was to keep farms in families, to round off land and improve stock. Courtship would be a protracted business while a young man worked for his inheritance, his share of what was to be divided and a daughter built up her bottom drawer or her sister became old enough to take her place in the kitchen. Her intended had plenty of time to discover that she could draw a fowl, make a cake, milk a cow, churn butter and run a dairy. Her education was invariably a practical one. There were few textbooks of any sort. Books on cookery, such as they were, were more often the work of men than of women. One of the eighteenth-century instructors of women whose work was handed down to the women of Queen Victoria's day couldn't help but tell them not to value their sex 'upon an embroidered gown' but urge them 'to more useful endeavours'. Although the female might be thought by some to be 'inferior in their intellectuals' to the other sex, yet in the sublimest part of humanity he could not really dispute their equality. It was surely no wonder that literate woman smiled encouragingly upon John Stuart Mill.

Before a young woman married a farmer she did well to know how to deal with a pig. This involved salting its hams. It also required her to know how to make brawn from its head, use its blood and intestines to make sausage and black puddings, to render its fat and store the lard, to smoke its whole side, minus the head, in the chimney, having lit a fire with oak chippings and sawdust. When she cured the ham she would spend an hour or two every day rubbing in a mixture of ordinary brine and saltpetre with perhaps a little brown sugar, some molasses or honey, depending upon her mother's recipe. When she helped to pluck and dress scores of Michaelmas and Christmas fowl she might trim the combs of the cockerels and blanch them for stewing, or cut out the tongues of her ducks and geese. These she would stew and flavour with essence of ham and a few herbs. It took fifty tongues to make a small dish! The essential thing in all this was frugality and frugality was inborn in women, particularly countrywomen. Throughout the past there had been echoes of famine in different parts of the world, although there had been no real famine in Britain between the sixteenth and nineteenth centuries.

Beer-brewing was another domestic enterprise which a woman might put her hand to in a household where labourers had always been accustomed to so much ale to quench their thirst, not just at harvest or haymaking, but all the year round. Recipes were outsize ones, like the barrels the beer was put into—five quarters of malted barley, eighteen pounds of hops or more! Brewing was done in October after the barley was harvested. The beer was allowed to stand until spring when the tun was vented and a second ferment encouraged. The beer was ready for drinking by September. The woman who wasn't required to make beer almost certainly made wine from cowslips, elderflowers, elderberries, damsons, raspberries or gilliflowers; but if the household was a temperance one she knew a dozen ways of preparing flesh or fowl, rabbit, pigeon, hare, the breasts of rooks shot in the rookery outside her door, crayfish from the brook—everything and anything her sporting family brought to the kitchen. Things that couldn't be dried and smoked would be preserved in clarified butter. The industrious Mrs Giles or her daughter even potted salt butter for the winter months when there was a shortage not only of cream but of milk. They were ready for every feast with things they had laid away. Cakes and puddings were made to keep for the better part of a year. They pickled pork, or green walnuts (while a darning needle could still be pushed through them). They even made their own vinegar, using a gallon of spring water and a couple of pounds of raisins left to sit in a stone vessel in the sun as they did in Portugal, but without raisins they would pickle things in gooseberry vinegar made in a similar way and using brown sugar to 'feed' the fermentation.

The family's ailments were the concern of an almost indestructible woman who had little time to be ill herself. She treated them as her own mother had treated the family, with purges, brimstone and treacle for impurities of the blood, castor oil, senna pods and later on, syrup of figs for more persistent constipation. A boil would be drawn by steaming a bottle. Toothache generally had to wait for the travelling tooth-puller. Bread poultices, linseed poultices, poultices of herbs relieved aches, sprains, strains and bronchial congestion. Old grandma, if she still lived, could be consulted over fevers and would produce out of her long memory a recipe for 'plague water' distilled from rosemary, rue, marigold, celandine, wormwood, agrimony, butterbur, peony or betony. The herbalist was held in greater respect than any surgeon, perhaps because it was easier to see the knife's failure and there was mystery in a cureall. People swore by the wart-charmer or the old woman who recommended comfrey for every kind of physical injury, external and internal. Old people carried half a dozen charms that kept rheumatism at bay. Arthritis has undoubtedly a lot to do with mental outlook although it has an undeniable physical manifestation. What the old people passed on to the unsophisticated simple countryfolk of the nineteenth century was the essential ingredient of every prescription, every formula for curing the body—faith. To believe in a cure is so important that without it almost every drug on a prescription is useless. The wart-charm has been simulated with X-ray, the lamp left on in so many cases and unpowered in as many, with the same percentage of success in either case—exactly half the number 'treated'! The countrywoman had more than faith, however. She had a great inheritance of superstition. It coloured life and told her it was bad luck to throw away bread, to hear a crowing hen, to see a black bird settle on the roof, to put an owl out of the chimney, to accept a hare shot at twilight. There was no end to the evil that might befall an ignorant non-believer, or people who paid no heed to the repeated advice of their elders. Old women were all witches. The seventh son of the seventh son was fey. There was a message in the playing cards, the palm of a woman's hand, the tea-leaves she swilled from her teacup. A child born with a caul on its head would never drown! Belief in things out of this world and beyond reason was inherited. The parson had long ago learned not to contradict too forcibly and to do his best to channel superstition into something a little more acceptable to the church. The church had always had a firm hold on the farming community and maintained it both spiritually and materially in the nineteenth century, even when, as Cobbett noted, the rector hobnobbed with his betters. Church on Sunday brought out the pony and the gig and the woman was able to lay aside her apron and put on her best dress. Fashion could hardly be the cornerstone of life in farming communities. Even the best dress was sober and practical. Cromwell's influence persisted among yeomen and tenant farmers. Their wives wore dresses that didn't need to be hoisted but covered their stout buttoned boots. Theirs was a sober, dignified, rather stiff-backed generation. Their clothes were designed to last a good part of a lifetime. They went squeakily to their pew and squeakily back up the aisle. They held their Bibles in their hands and tried hard to remember the main points of the sermon. They drove home looking at their neighbours' fields and frowned at those who had obviously not been at church. In the evening they might sit in the parlour and sing hymns together to piano accompaniment, but the songs of Stephen Foster, even 'Old Black Joe', were not for the sabbath.

Home entertainment tended to be homemade, self-amusement rather than ready-made, although the magic lantern was already in being and, with or without commentary, provided visions of the broader landscapes of foreign countries. The kaleidoscope delighted women as well as children for Sir David Brewster's invention produced ever-changing patterns in most beautiful colours. Edison would soon be demonstrating how recorded music could be reproduced and the phonograph was on the way to provide the first canned music. The old clockwork music box that tinkled out well-known tunes would be put away. Victorian woman was as eager for novelty as any generation of women had ever been and she was ready to give up her parlour exhibits of stuffed birds and animals in glass cases for pug dogs and white delft ornaments or the piano for the pianola when the Americans sent that over. There was a paraffin cooking stove on the way. She was ready to have the iron range pulled out and carted to the scrap iron merchant. She was more and more conscious of being beyond the pale, beyond the reach of installations provided in cities and towns. She would never ride in a tramcar, cook with town gas or see the world lit up at night. Being outside fashion troubled her a great deal more than her husband, but neither of them dreamed how much the world would change in half a century, when the mechanics and the inventors really set their minds to improving what they had already achieved. No one would have to carry water from the well, trim a wick or carry a lantern to the shippon, catch a horse to go to market or look through a quaint old postcard viewer to see Niagara or the Eiffel Tower. No woman would need to know how to cure a ham, preserve fruit, or even bake a cake. Progress would take care of it all, and what had been the vital know-how of generations would slip out of the heads of the old people and never be needed again. No one would sit and sing hymns on Sunday—or bother to cook a meal so that the day of rest could be spent going to church. The old order would go. There would be no time to look back to see the going of it. Life is change and there is no altering the fact.

9

Trades and Callings

S INCE WHAT happens in the main centres of population affects the population as a whole, and social change is a continual process, the structure of the rural community has changed. It may be that for a time the modification in a way of weaving or spinning didn't really reduce the rural population but simply reduced the circumstances of those who had been cottage weavers or used the spinning wheel. Ultimately however such ripples changed the way of life, darkened the future and the prospects of younger people who might have found a living. There were a number of trades and crafts that were a long-established integral part of the fabric of rural life, thatching, for instance, the wheelwright's trade, coopering, wagon and coach-building, black-smithing, the trade of the mason and the wall-builder. Some of these trades and crafts in fact enjoyed temporary booms. Some were like the thatcher's which really had nowhere to go except as maintenance of old roofs and the very occasional, somewhat rare use of reed or wheat straw in a new structure. There never had been a boom in the building trade beyond towns in which industry had already begun to flourish, and industry flourished as a result of improved communications systems—the canals and railways. The resulting traffic was two-way. It enabled manufactured goods and the produce of the surrounding agricultural area to be shipped off to larger cities and the export market. It brought in new materials, bricks to compete with local stone, tiles and slate to underline the fact that thatch would burn. The slater or tiler could cover a roof faster than a thatcher, but things that are old have been time-tested. The old people who lived in daub and wattle, half-timbered Elizabethan cottages, or larger rambling places with ancient black thatch, knew what a wonderful insulation thatch was. It breathed, and a man lay snug in his four-poster listening to sparrows that invariably found a way through the eaves' netting to warm roosting places. Thatch, however, depended upon reeds or the best wheat straw being available when a roof had to be renewed. It was a material that needed to be protected not only from birds, but from rats and mice. It had to be watched in dry weather in case of sparks from the chimney. That it made a picturesque roof was a by-product. Slate could shed water without ever rotting, though a house would never be as warm. A more solid roof was made with tiles, and both bricks and tiles could be brought from the clay bed areas where brick-making had been the main source of supply of building material.

The thatcher didn't so much watch the decline of his craft as the change in technique, but with the wheelwright it was different. Since the days of the chariot the wheel had been in ever greater demand. Mathematicians had gone into raptures about its perfection and the sublime inspiration that had led to its invention, as though man might have dreamed of fur coats before he knew the cold or sowing crops before he had come through bitter winters! The wheel was refined more and more as the roads over which it rolled were improved. Along with lighter wheels for the 'post chariot' the wheelwright had to give a lot of his time to the making of wheels for wagons and haywains. Even the post chariot was a lumbering affair that gave its wretched passengers a great shaking up at times and creaked and jolted its way through the mire, relying on the stout wheels with which the wheelwright had equipped it—and the convenient situation of men of that craft along the route. Even so, the coach would come to a halt for reasons other than a broken wheel. The grease that lubricated the axle would burn away. The hub would bind and the coach would be left isolated out there in the open country, at the mercy, if not of highwaymen, of the weather, which could be as hostile as the countryside itself. In 1792 a gentleman named Collinge contributed his bit to the smoother passage of the mail and the comfort of its passengers by inventing an oil box axle that carried three months' supply of oil. Coaches might be held up by blizzards and flood, but there was no longer any danger of a smoking axle bringing the thing to a standstill more effectively than the driver hauling on a brake or dropping a skid shoe to slow his vehicle on its way down a steep hill. Whatever happened along the mail route was grist to the mill for the coach-builder, the wheelwright, the smith, and even the ostler who changed the teams and carried the luggage of the passengers when an overnight stay was being made.

The heavy post chariot was really built like a sturdy fishing smack. It battled through conditions almost as bad as those faced by the fishermen. The first mail coach ran between London and Bath in 1784 and its successful operation, backed up by changes of horses at inns along the way and the tradesmen to make repairs, renail shoes or change a wheel, inspired the establishment of forty-two coach routes before that century was at an end. The wheelwright would have made his living no matter what because he was a craftsman in wood, able to turn his hand to other things. The post chariot and the post chaise, whether they were driven from the box or manned by a postilion, guaranteed work in the trade but private carriages were in fashion more and more with road improvement. The post chariot and post chaise, which were really a scaling-up of the sedan chair set on wheels, undoubtedly inspired Lord Brougham when he ordered a carriage to his own design in 1838. The brougham was drawn by one horse. Not everyone wanted to travel by the stage or the carrier's cart and a one-horse carriage must have been a status symbol for all those who could build a carriage house and stable. While many gentlemen were content to rattle along the road in a fly, a one-horse hackney which might be hired or privately owned, there were much more ostentatious conveyances for those of higher social orders. When his lordship and her ladyship drove to church on Sunday, graciously acknowledging the homage of the tenantry, they might ride in a phaeton drawn by a pair of greys. The landau was even grander as a piece of four-wheeled transport, likely to make dog cart and rickety fly draw to one side. In the landau the passengers could have the best of both worlds by virtue of hoods which, raised singly, sheltered a lady's hat from the breeze and kept the dust from her eyes, or, both raised, made the thing into a closed carriage. The barouche was only a short step from the landau, which was of French origin. Gigs, dogcarts and flys were mainly for parsons, yeomen farmers and country lawyers.

With all this horse-drawn rolling stock of one kind and another, no one could possibly have foreseen the day when the wheelwright's trade would be a curiosity, almost a by-gone business. Even the man busy in his shed trying to make some kind of locomotive out of the internal combustion engine had so many problems to solve that he couldn't make up his mind about wheels, whether they would be iron or wood, have solid tyres or no tyres at all. The steam engine, a highly efficient thing when stationary, had no help but to carry along with it massive iron wheels once it became a locomotive. The man who dreamt of the automobile was likely to hanker after light wooden wheels or wheels with wooden rims.

The wheelwright's finest work went into the making of more delicate wheels, finer spokes, tall wheels that added to the elegance of the landau and the barouche, handsome little wheels for the dogcart. The coach-builder's design went with them. The coach-painter painted them chocolate and yellow, lined them with gold. They spun until their colours blended and their varnish flashed in the spring sunshine. Elegance was the aim of the wealthy, and elegance pleased the craftsman and the artist more than anything else. Even the coachman dressed like a gentleman in a top hat. His livery was grand. Basically, however, the wheelwright was concerned with practical things, the selection of the right wood, the soundness and solidity of the way in which his wheel was made, whether it was man-high or small, had eight spokes or a dozen. When the wheel was completed it still had to be shod. This was really a smith's work for an iron wheelshod had to be made precisely so that it would come hot from the fire, just scorching the wheel before it was cooled and shrunk on to its circumference. A too large wheelshod would simply rattle off the wheel the first time it rolled. A too small one would burn the wood away without ever settling in place. The smith and the wheelwright knew their materials and smiths regularly employed to put iron on wheels would do so on a specially made circular stone base which enabled the smith and his helpers to work round the wheel (two or three men if they were needed), lowering the hot iron rim on to the wheel while another hurried round it, pouring water to shrink the wheelshod evenly in place. When this was done all that was needed was a final tap or two perhaps, and the coach-painter would have his wheels to undercoat and rub down, paint and varnish. There was no shortage of work for a wheel-wright business. Apprentices were taken in to learn the trade. The railway couldn't run everywhere, even if it would soon create a crisis for the mail and there would be an outcry about the escalating cost of postage. The wheelwright looked at the increasing number of vehicles drawn by horses, even horse buses, took comfort from the sight of them. The blacksmith, certainly the shoeing smith, might well have had occasional nightmares filled with rushing horse teams and bouncing wheels. Every horse had four legs apiece and on the hard roads wore out their shoes faster than ever. There was also as great a demand as ever for everyday ironwork.

The smith's calling was as ancient as that of the wheelwright, although down through the centuries he might have been more con-cerned with armour and horses of war than the shoeing of draught animals. A team of oxen hauling a wagon might or might not have worn shoes. Drovers certainly had occasion to enlist the shoeing smith's help when they brought their beasts to assembly places ready for the long trek south. The smith was, however, handyman to the community in general. They relied upon him to make bolts for their doors, bars for their windows, to mend whatever iron implements became unusable. He had made a snatching hook for the poacher, a mantrap for the landowner. He tempered and fettled tools that cut, reforged the quarryman's jumper drills, his picks and other tools. He was of course, more than a mender. He was a craftsman as well as a tradesman and he had secrets to impart to the apprentice he took into his service. While the village might be his audience when he put shoes on a horse or laid out the iron framework of his lord-ship's new gates, when the secrets of his craft might be at risk he closed his doors and covered his work as all craftsmen, workers in metal and wood, invariably did. In the age of the draught horse an endless queue of horses might stand outside the smithy door waiting for sets of shoes. The smith was never paid very much de-spite the need for his work and in the country, if not in the town, there was often not much silver, let alone gold about. He would take payment in kind. Barter had always been part of the commercial lifeblood of the rural community. Although the smith had to buy his iron, and mouldboards were what might nowadays be called 'bought out parts', a tradesmen doing regular work for farmers would take a bag of flour in payment for two or three sets of shoes, a sack of oatmeal perhaps, some swedes, potatoes, butter and eggs. Particularly in the middle years of the nineteenth century these things were as welcome as silver.

Inevitably when the mechanical reaper came into fashion the smith who had a certain mechanical ability often had to leave his smithy and go where the work was. A corn or hay reaper could be hoisted on to a wagon. The binder had transport wheels but no farmer was very happy to see his most important implements taken out of the field when the corn was ripe and waiting to be cut. The machine could hardly have been expected to take to every sort of land. Where the ground was hard to plough it was also hard to mow because of stones and boulders. The nuts and bolts, the braces and brackets, would be shaken loose and the clattering monster come to a standstill in the middle of the cut. Farmers, like blacksmiths, had to learn a little about the function of different parts of the binder. There had been nothing quite so complicated on the field before and anything with a number of working parts suffers more wear and tear and encounters more breakdowns. There were other adjustments that had to be made before difficult fields could be cut and the problem of suitable labour to handle the machine and do the job bothered the farmer with the newfangled harvesting machine. He generally solved it by climbing up into the driving seat himself. His nightmare was that it would bog down and come to a permanent halt with all the mowers, the lifters and tyers of sheaves gone over the hill. The thing was a sort of mechanical octopus to those who first saw it, as awe-inspiring as the steam train or the great, tall chimneyed engine that hauled the threshing mill. When the binder did dig itself in like an obstinate mule the smith came hurrying with his bag of tools and spanners to crawl under it, through it and over it, diagnosing its sickness or its mechanical weakness. The makers of the machines were reluctant to admit that it wasn't the perfect thing for steep hills or boggy ground. It wasn't their fault that it took a long time to get a spare part, for there were few implement makers within easy reach of the distraught farmer, and until machines of reliable design were in general use the smith had to effect what repairs he could. Occasionally the smith had no help but to drag the machine away to his forge and make a new part while the corn bleached, apples dropped in the orchard and the first leaves began to fall from the tree. Harvest was a long-drawn-out business in any case. It became a disaster when a farmer had to go back to the old way. There really was no going back. The die was cast, and cast as much for the worker in iron as it was for the harvester and the ploughman.

The Victorians were great patrons of the smith and probably appreciated ironwork more than any generation before or since. They loved ornamentation, scrolls and whorls. They also loved things to be solid and functional, made to last for ever, as though there would be no new fashion, no modification. The lampposts to light the town with gas were the work of the iron foundry, heavy and almost indestructible. Railings and gates, seats, hinges, brackets made by the smith were all of the same style, made to last like the houses that were being put up, the public buildings and somewhat grim nonconformist churches and chapels that went with them. The nineteenth century was a great time for the entrepreneur and the investor in schemes to quarry stone and slate. There was a boom in the slate industry towards the end of the century. All at once slate seemed to be needed everywhere. It covered the roofs of expanding towns where industry began to flourish. The slater nailed down slate here, there and everywhere, as fast as roof timbers could be put up. Where slate could be quarried slate towns grew to house the quarry workers as in North Wales. The finest blue Welsh slate was shipped off, trundled out of the quarries on narrow gauge railways, loaded on boats and cheaply and quickly moved to its ultimate destination, leaving only two problems, like the coal industry, mountains of waste and men with lung trouble! The building of so many houses on the perimeter of towns did nothing for the mason who had hitherto been one of the most important craftsmen. Building in stone was going out of fashion. It was a slower process in any case. It involved the cutting of stone in the quarry and the movement of more massive material to the scene of operations. Brick had always more than held its own in those parts of the country where good local stone was not to be had, but even in the north, where building in stone had been a tradition, the mason's work began a slow decline. There was still work for wall builders, however, particularly drystone wallers and men skilled in building earth and stone. The enclosure of land, the regulation of what was grazing right and what was not common, had kept the wallers in work. They built in stone generally because the stone was there, under their feet in the form of boulders turned up by the plough, carted to its perimeter by the man cultivating the land. It was a skilled trade and like most trades in the country, one at which a man took his time. It was paid for by the chain and wallers worked as a team, building what were sometimes called 'march' walls, slightly higher walls dividing one parish from the next or one man's farm from his neighbour's, and walls of perhaps four to five feet to separate pasture from arable land within the marches. A good drystone wall depended upon the grading of the stone tipped along the line to make it. As a rule it would be built considerably broader or wider at the base than at the top and if properly made, slightly incurved to stand the force of the gale and deflect the wind. The expert waller using glacial boulders and not quarried or more or less square-sided rock, would lift his stone, quickly look at it and roll it in his hands before laying it in place. In doing this he would ensure its fitting in place and settling in the niche or depression he had chosen. The finished wall would have to withstand not just the gale or the ravages of the weather, which might wash away the subsoil, but a stampeding bullock or a determined black-faced ram rushing up it to break out. A great many people born in the twentieth century stand and stare with amazement at the work of the long-dead dry-stone wallers who built walls up what seemed to be sheer hills. Who paid for the work and who carried the millions of tons of rock and boulders used in the walls? A lot of the stone was close at hand. What wasn't had to be carted or sledged to the site. Wallers had to have no thought of tomorrow, next week or next month, and they were paid a very small wage, often living and working as employees on the vast estate their walls delineated.

The work of the drystone waller was a far cry from the mason's craft, of course. Somewhere in between was the waller working with limestone, using quarried stone as the outer shell of his wall which was mortar bound, and large quantities of limestone rubble as the core of the wall. So long as the mortar remains intact this wall is a much better one than a drystone construction, even one built of rock slabs and segments of quarried stone perhaps, but the penetration of water and the effects of low temperature often break the mortar away, a coping stone is displaced, ivy or elderberry grows and its roots or the roots of valerian expand and the rubble core begins to spill out. Perhaps the most effective wall is one still to be seen in many parts of the country where surface boulders were not too plentiful and ordinary drystone walling wasn't possible. The sod and boulder wall, although it takes up more room, seems to stand firm for ever and only a bulldozer might break it down, especially where thorns and furze manage to take root in the earthwork.

While the mason was employed on the mansion and the more important sort of yeoman farmer's dwelling, lesser craftsmen built in undressed stone obtainable close at hand. The fashion for farm houses and farm buildings to be of brick in one part of the country and stone in another was predetermined by the availability of material. Where there was no good local stone, bricks might be had or could be carted. The rough stone of so many northern slate-roofed farms is often more than three feet thick, mortared to make it weatherproof on the outside and then coated with limewash to preserve the waterproofing. In some places half-timbering enabled the builder to economize in brick or stone. Wattle and daub was an old technique. In slate areas a gable might be entirely covered with slated battens but slate made a very cold house unless extra insulation was devised on the inside of the timbers. Few architects were ever consulted when a farmhouse was built. Indeed most farmhouses were renovations of older, and still older buildings that grew and sprawled and lurched until they had to be rescued and buttressed, shored up and strengthened. The know-how came out of the distant past when a roof-tree was a roof tree and there was no such thing as a triangle of forces, or no one had a name for it!

There was another important craft or trade that was an integral part of life, both in the country and the town—the cooper's. Just as the business of communications and transport was a world of wheels and horseshoes, the domestic scene and rural industry was very much a world of casks and tuns, of tubs and firkins, churns and barrels of all sorts—'slack casks' for dry goods, 'tight casks' for liquids. Everywhere they brewed their own local beer and made their own cider. The cooper had to provide the casks. There was also what was called white coopering which involved the use of soft wood, largely for buckets and tubs and temporary containers for food. In hardwood coopering the best casks were made from oak. The late nineteenth century saw coopering being done by machines but there were also hand coopers and they were as important to the country community as carpenters and joiners whose workplaces were outside the town. Coopers needed both skill and equipment to make casks of different sizes, if not skill of as high a degree as the wheelwright's or the smith's, a very special technique. A cask was not simply a set of slats bent to form a barrel, but slats of a dimension that would when steamed and roped in place, produce a precise conical form of equal circumference at either end. To make a tight cask the already shaped staves were assembled on their ends inside a special frame. Each stave before being stood in the circular frame was already grooved to take the barrel ends. The ends were placed in position as the staves were drawn tight in temporary truss hoops of windlassed rope which tightened them as the steaming took place. A perfect oak cask would sit exactly on top of one previously completed, would roll across the floor as smoothly as a marble. Before the windlassed rope was slackened from the steamed barrel, the barrel had to be hooped with permanent iron hoops driven on from either end. This held the close-fitting staves together. The barrel was strong enough to be rolled down into a cellar when it held many gallons of beer or porter.

The man who went in for white coopering had fewer problems. He was not, after all, making casks in which spirits would have to age, or containers for things more valuable than swill, soapy water or bran, but white coopering, like ironmongery, was essential to a farm household. There was a continual need for tubs and buckets, buckets to draw water from the well and tubs in which potatoes or apples might be kept. The butter churn had to be a piece of tight coopering because it was the sort of equipment that needed to last a lifetime. Wherever local inns gave up making their own beer and beer-making moved to brewery premises coopers followed. Theirs was a very widespread trade, like the smith's. Like the smith too the 'trade' name was given many who followed it, and handed down with all the Smiths, Warreners, Cartwrights and Turners listed in directories today.

Less of a steady trade was the ancient one of tinker, tinsmith or tinkler. The tinker was generally an itinerant and more often than not, either a gypsy or of gypsy blood. Most heavy domestic utensils tended to be of iron. There were even heavy iron kettles on the hobs of farm ranges well into the present century, but copper and tin vessels were in use in the old days. Cheap tin kettles however only became readily available when machines were made in the Midlands to turn out tinware at high speed. Before mass production took over tinkers repaired kettles at the door. Tinning the inside of a copper kettle or teapot was an art. The utensil had to be heated before the solder was put into it, swilled round to coat the whole surface and then wiped out. The sad thing about a copper teapot was that it would oxidize and discolour. Worse still, it would pour a poisonous cup of tea. There were always such pots and pans to be mended and for a long time, itinerant tinkers to mend them. It was the habit of many of these so-called tradesmen to ply their trade only when there was no other work to be had. Between times they lived by their wits, poached or did casual work for farmers in whatever district they spent the season. The very old tinker generally despised the man who lived by his wits and preferred to tin or braze metal and repair domestic equipment. Alas for the genuine tinker, his fellow travellers always succeeded in getting themselves a bad name. The poor tinker was of the country, but never really belonged anywhere. His sons, if they did any sort of useful work at all, came to supervise their wives and children making clothes pegs, clothes props, baskets and other items of this kind. The nineteenth century was really more the age of iron than of copper. When tin trays and tin basins, baths, and kettles were finally piled high for the farmer's wife to buy on a market day they were so cheap that no one ever thought of having them repaired. These tin utensils were usually of such poor tin that they discoloured and rusted long before a tinker ever came on the scene to mend them. Early in the present century the last of the tinkers went rattling and jangling away, his craft finally abandoned. His skills were never to be revived in a generation that went from cheap tinware to aluminium and finally to plastic, which no one could repair.

What really hastened the decline in rural crafts and trades was the call for slightly different skills in other areas. This may not have applied to the tinker but it applied to the smith and the wheelwright.

There is always a need for manual skill that is a matter of individual talent for doing things with hand and eye. A wheelwright or a cooper was a skilled worker in wood. A smith was a man able to fashion things in iron and a passable mechanic. The nineteenth century needed these crafts in all parts of the country. The twentieth had less need of craft but required individuals with manual ability. Hands were needed in the factory, on the machine and even behind the wheel. Unfortunately for the son of the wheelwright, or the smith, the work he was asked to do gave no opportunity to create anything except a production total.

10

The Keeper's Kingdom

MOST of those who farmed land in the eighteenth and nineteenth century were tenants rather than freeholders and their inheritance was a feudal one with a lease which laid down the landowner's rights regarding game. A tenant could quite easily be put out. He could destroy vermin, but he must leave game strictly for the owner. He ploughed and sowed but if the squire chose to hunt or shoot there was nothing he could do to prevent him coming on the land with hounds, dogs and his retinue of keepers. The woods and even the meadows were the keeper's kingdom and the pattern had been there in the days of the Norman rulers to be imitated when later kings made grants of land with the right to hunt. The keeper was a man of influence because he had the ear of his master. He saw more than the bailiff or agent and a tenant who valued his lease did well to keep in his good books. A word from this formidable servant of the landowner and the lease might be refused. The killing of a hare would be regarded as a serious crime. A dog allowed to run loose in a wood was provocation. The keeper hardly needed to voice his displeasure. There was only one side of the fence so far as he was concerned. He lived in an estate cottage. He didn't own the gun he carried. The dog at his heel belonged to his master more often than not. The clothes he wore were bought for him and if he lost his place for a dereliction of duty he would join the paupers. Other landlords would turn him down. No tenant would offer him work on the farm. His job was uniquely fraught with difficulties because he was a man in the middle. If a season proved a disaster he might be dismissed whether he was really at fault or not. If poachers overcame his defences he was accused of not doing his job. The farmers feared and tolerated him. The labourers disliked him and he walked alone. If he drank, he drank alone. His job was to protect his master's interests, to prevent poaching, to destroy vermin, to rear birds as well as he could, and to acccompany his master when he went shooting. Game flourished only by the intervention of man trapping, snaring, shooting or poisoning predators. Trespass in pursuit of game was a serious offence and the poor were often hungry. The keeper's job was to keep them from helping themselves, for this was a shortcut to anarchy. Bringing poachers to book was one of the ways the unfortunate keeper could prove that he was doing his job, and when he did he had the backing of the magistrates who were always men of property and often landowners themselves. The penalties were severe because fines were useless when the offenders were penniless. It was not unusual for a poacher to be sent to prison for two or three months, even six months, for shooting a pheasant or netting a hare. Persistent offenders faced transportation in the eighteenth century, though this punishment was abandoned later on in the nineteenth. The mantrap had its day and it too, was finally outlawed, but poaching remained a serious crime and it was important that the keeper should be as good at catching offenders as he was at putting out game!

When game-rearing for organized shoots really began to develop the keeper's work was judged not only by the stock of birds he could show in the season but by that grisly exhibition called the gibbet. Here, on a rail fence or frame, he displayed the vermin he had trapped and shot. A score of rotting crows advertised themselves to the landowner when he visited his keeper. He saw that his man had been diligently destroying the carrion crow, the rat, the vole, jay, magpie, hawk, polecat, stoat, weasel, the barn owl, the tawny owl, even the moorhen and the domestic cat! There was hardly a bird bigger than a thrush that didn't fall to the gun in the interest of the pampered gamebird. No one talked of ecology in Victorian times. The poletrap was a common device for perching owls and greedy magpies. It caught the falcon too, but in a war there are always unfortunate casualties. Strychnine was a great standby. It didn't matter if the farmer's dog died from eating a bait. His dog should never have been roaming free in the first place. It was no wonder that the keeper was unpopular with tenants. His image was the worst possible when he happened to be an incomer engaged for that very reason. Landowners would often seek keepers from the other end of the country to make sure that they had no connections among the locals. The unfortunate incomer was compelled to battle on in the face of a hostility he could never hope to break down.

What happened in the shooting field was governed in the eighteenth century by the kind of gun a man was able to use to shoot game. The flintlock was all there was, and it was a far from satisfactory fowling piece. It was heavy. The powder with which it was primed was exposed in the pan in which the spark from the strike of the flint fell. It often misfired for one reason or another. On a wet day it was an almost useless weapon. On a damp day it was erratic. Flashes in the pan without ignition were common. When the long-barrelled, clumsy gun fired there was a plume, or even a pall of smoke, which often obscured the bird that had been aimed at. It was no small feat to receive and discharge a second shot at the same covey of birds while they were still in range. This was probably all in the interests of conservation even in a day when wildfowl flourished.

The excursion after game tended to be a leisurely one. Water spaniels ploughed into reeds and the squire waited for a bird to be flushed, fired his flintlock and handed it to his man to have it recharged. The man carried the bag and the second fowling piece, and controlled the assortment of retrievers, pointers or marking dogs that were part of the business. Organized drives with such unreliable weapons were not very productive until a gentleman of the cloth, the Rev Alexander Forsyth, patented a little thing called a percussion cap. The percussion cap made the flint and the pan obsolete. A hammer replaced the flint mechanism to detonate a charge contained in the cap. The cap was fixed on a nipple screwed in the barrel of the gun. Its detonation ignited the powder behind the wad and the charge of shot. It was all so simple and it was the answer to a prayer, but like a great many other new devices the Rev Forsyth's patent was a long time on file before the army appreciated its significance. By misfires and flashes in the pan the flintlock had undoubtedly cost many a brave soldier his life when cavalry charged with sabres. It was thirty years before the percussion cap musket replaced the flintlock as a military weapon. The Rev Forsyth's patent was dated 1807. The battle of Waterloo was fought in 1815. The War Office evidently had no enthusiasm for newfangled things! Bravery won battles.

The sporting world was less conservative in its outlook however, and gunsmiths were busy on the percussion cap muzzleloader. Joe Manton, one of the great gunsmiths of the nineteenth century, not only produced some beautiful percussion cap single-barrelled guns but patented an improvement of his own—a centre rib which enabled the side-by-side double-barrelled percussion cap gun to be used. His patron was the celebrated Colonel Peter Hawker, a military man obsessed with wildfowling and shooting in general. The side-by-side gun was the delight of the shooting man. Its hammers were graceful. Its engraving a work of art. Its barrels were Damascus patterned by winding a fine iron strip round a mandrel. There remained one further major improvement—to dispense with the percussion cap altogether and combine cap, powder and charge in a cartridge loaded at the breech. The advent of the Anson and Deeley action—a gastight breech action—finally made this possible. The ramrod and the cap were no longer needed. A man could load and fire much faster than ever before and highly sophisticated designs were worked upon by famous gunsmiths who took up where Manton had left off to produce the hammerless gun and finally the hammerless ejector. There had never been such a time for the makers of sporting guns. If this was the golden age of fox-hunting men it was also the golden age of the shooting man. The improved gun meant a revolution in the gamekeeper's world. Where he had operated largely as a policeman and a destroyer of vermin he now needed to rear game much more intensively. The shooting man was able to travel. The world had contracted a little. A train to the far north made it easy to get to the grouse moor. The wooded country of the Midlands, the southern counties and the rich land of Norfolk were ideal for game cultivation. For the unfortunate keeper, however, there were few shortcuts and innovations. He achieved his norm by catching up pheasants and having them lay in pens so that he could gather their eggs. The hen pheasant broods eggs less diligently than the domestic chicken. She will desert her clutch with little provocation. The broody hen will sit through thick and thin whether on her own eggs or the eggs of another species. All the keeper needed was enough broody hens, a set of coops and a pen in which he could rear the chicks. It was always a tall order nevertheless, to find enough broody hens and produce young poults on a scale large enough to meet the demand. Although a broody hen may cover more eggs than a hen pheasant there is a limit to the number she may successfully incubate. To stock his covers for a season the keeper might hope for a thousand poults. The fertility of the eggs set, the losses in the process of brooding the chicks, and the final toll from predators of one sort or another would boil the numbers down—ninety per cent at best of the eggs set. Perhaps eighty per cent survival among the chicks and a final figure nearer half a thousand than a thousand young pheasants established in the woods. The final product was only achieved after the most arduous struggle to care for and feed the young birds. This meant a catch-up of hen pheasants and a few cock birds as early in the year as possible so that egg gathering could begin as soon as laying was properly under way. The watering and feeding of broody hens kept men and boys busy, but the real pressure of work was when the chicks began to hatch. From this time on there would be no respite for anyone between first light and the fall of night. The establishment of young pheasants in the woods where they would still be handfed was, and still is, half of the secret of game-stocking. There had to be an improvement in method and the answer finally came with the incubator, an oil-fired installation which replaced the broody hen. Even with this machine there were still losses and the chicks had to be kept at brood heat while they gained strength. The estate with electricity finally brought the whole thing in under cover by using the electric incubator and brooder. The more highly-developed incubators not only controlled humidity, essential to the chick breaking the shell, but turned the eggs as a bird would have turned them while sitting. All of this undoubtedly began with the patenting of the percussion cap and the development of the modern shotgun. In those days before game-rearing became the accepted thing the flintlock had been in keeping with the survival rate in the wild pheasant—three fullgrown birds from a clutch of eggs.

In the course of their work to meet the demands of the shooting fraternity old keepers became naturalists of a sort. They might not have been too aware of the dependence of one species upon another and the real effect of killing off a particular bird or quadruped, but they learned the ways of the birds they nursed and cultivated. They discovered what they ate, where they thrived best, and what plants or seeds attracted them. Mixtures of seed were one of secrets which old keepers passed on to their sons. By planting crops like sunflower, for instance, they ensured that pheasants didn't wander in search of food. This made them easier to watch over and protect. Feeding the ground was a very old device and one of which the poacher was equally well aware. The hand-fed bird is inclined to be tame and it falls prey not just to the fox, the dog or the feral cat but to the poacher. On the other hand, the very tameness of the hand-reared pheasant makes it possible to drive it over the guns. It is fed and walked or driven in so that it is there to be driven out. The man who preserves game for shooting hardly dares count the cost. It is impossible to sell a brace of pheasants to a dealer and show a profit. 'Bang goes sixpence,' the old shooting man would say, 'and down comes a pound'—it cost forty times as much as the cartridge to put the bird in the air to be shot. A brace of pheasants generally cost the cook a little less than half a sovereign at that time. Few sporting gentlemen would have cared to talk about the cost of sport in strict terms of outlay and return. It wasn't done. The pheasant was a bird in the air or a bird on the plate, previously hung until it became high, and accompanied by a bottle of good red wine!

While they were solving the keeper's problem with the incubator, experts of another sort were giving attention to the ammunition used to shoot game. Black powder left smoke in the air. Moreover, it lacked power compared with some of the powders being tested and it fouled the barrels of the gun. The new powders were more efficient ballistically. The only trouble was that the old mandrel-wound Damascus barrel couldn't cope with such heavy loads. The gun had to be modified once more and fitted with drawn steel tube barrels that wouldn't blow up like a balloon under pressure and send a fragment of iron to chip a lump from a man's head or put his eye out. With this the gameshot was finally completely equipped for the field. The keeper could marshal his beaters (the local farmers and trusted tenants) and drive his host of tame pheasants out of the wood and over the tallest elms and beeches to be shot at by the guns away down below. Ritual shooting with fixed angles and a peculiar mindlessness didn't trouble the banker or the stockbroker. The keeper had finally become a kind of farmer, rearing his stock, feeding and protecting it for the greater part of the year before finally delivering it to the guns. It had all come a long, long way from the Bewick engraving of the shooter in his top hat priming his fowling piece, with hunting dogs swarming all round him and snipe whipping away over the marsh. In the intervening years even that other romantic figure—the old poacher—had had his image changed and tarnished. He was recognized as a thief and this of course, he always had been, although it would never have entered his head to think that he was. The bird he contemplated flew free. It roosted in the tree he could see from his cottage window. Sometimes it even walked across his potato patch. He saw it out there on the golden stubbles of autumn. He heard it crow when it was twilight and it was part of the world in which he lived like the rook, the magpie and the screeching jay. No one claimed any of these. Why should the pheasant belong to a man who reared it and then set it free? If he had a backyard fowl he kept it in his backyard, and locked it in against the fox. If he wanted to eat it he put it in his pot. The landowner claimed a lot of things he seemed to have no God-given right to claim and the keeper was his tool. When times were hard a man had to live as best he could. He could make a few shillings catching the bird in the bush or setting a wire. What great loss was that to a man who had more than he could ever want and drove home in a fine carriage? The game was really a very old one, older than civilization, but in the eighteenth and nineteenth century it had really come down to a battle between the hungry man and the landlord's minion, the keeper. If it wasn't possible to get at the pheasant with a gun there were other ways. If the keepers were out diversions could be created so that a wood could be raided. If they were in, someone could be posted to see that they remained indoors while the birds were caught and there were dozens of ways of catching them, with catapults and throwing sticks, with nets and snares and sulphur fumes as well as with the lurcher dog. They could be trapped and they could be doped or they could be taken with bird-lime made by boiling hollybark with plaster added to it. Sometimes the keeper could be bribed and sometimes he could be intimidated.

Occasionally he stood his ground and they exchanged shots. Sometimes he came with helpers to back him up. The village constable was on his side.

Poaching gangs were almost always incomers, miners or unemployed men who came out from the town to take what game they could by force if this proved necessary. The miners were always gamblers and not in the least afraid of physical encounters. A few keepers and estate workers were nothing to be afraid of. If they were surprised when they were busy knocking light-dazzled pheasants off their perches they faced the enemy and fired back at him. There would often be casualties on both sides and sometimes a man would be killed. This was the risk. The reward made it worthwhile. The excitement was a bonus. It was a battlefield which the landlord avoided, though he would expect to hear how it had gone in the morning if he heard shots fired in the night. An estate that lost the day and failed to stop such invasions would soon be overrun. The keeper's life would become impossible. The stock would be depleted and the shooting reduced to nothing. Occasionally a keeper joined the opposition and made a deal with the poachers or sold what he could of the game he could catch to dealers or hoteliers. The sale of game by an estate keeper is a transaction to which his employer must consent. Without this authority the sale is illegal. The vendor and the purchaser have both committed an offence. It is to prevent this happening that game dealers require to be licensed. One shot pheasant looks like another and the source of supply has to be recorded. The poacher, of course, puts his name to nothing and the purchaser knows the bird has been poached even when it carries the marks of shot. There never was a professional poacher who bothered to buy a licence to shoot game or a crooked game dealer who thought to ask where the birds came from. The old poacher with whom the bench sometimes began to deal leniently, recognizing him as incorrigible and unable to curb his instinct to pursue game whatever the penalties, has faded from the scene. His place is taken by an entirely different character, a sort of hit-and-run poacher who shoots from a car, uses a small-bore rifle and doesn't stand upon the order of his going. The keeper despairs of catching him in the act and fears much more the gang, no longer composed of miners seeking excitement or the unemployed, but a much more ruthless collection of commercial desperados who stop at nothing.

The change in the sporting scene in the twentieth century is a radical one. Like the old hunting squire, the landowner has been forced to cut his shooting coat according to his cloth. He can rarely afford not to consider what his pheasant costs him! His accountant reminds him of self-indulgence. The Inland Revenue may assess his shooting rights and take it all into the reckoning. He may call his keeper a woodman and move items from one column to another, but his final resort is to let the whole shooting match to the syndicate, the keeper and his rearing field along with it. The syndicate has become rather like the subscriber's hunt. It pays the bills. It provides the wages of the keeper and chick crumbs, the feeders and the waterdishes, the incubators and brooders when these wear out. It shoots half a dozen times a year and leaves the keeper to get on with his job. He is, after all, supposed to know his business. They judge him by the bag and sell the bag to help pay his wages. The estate itself has been eroded by taxation and death duties. Its boundaries have contracted. There may no longer be an under-keeper or a boy to help with rearing birds. That kind of thing began to go out with the heated wall on which the peaches were grown and the day when his lordship waited for his liveried footman to open the door of his carriage before he stepped down. The keeper's kingdom is now no place for the absolute monarch. He spends a lot of his time winning the goodwill of the farmers. He doesn't shoot the hawk any more. He is inclined to think the stoat and the weasel aren't as great a menace as his father thought them. He is doubtful of the wisdom of his son following in his footsteps and wonders if anyone will be shooting in fifty years time. And he is probably right to wonder, for things are not what they were and never will be the same again. The shotgun is more of a bank robber's weapon. The great English gun makers have almost all gone out of business. The chap, mass-produced foreign gun is a drug on the market. A man needs a shotgun certificate to possess a shotgun—which keeps the clerks busy and does nothing to stop the bank robber.

There was always another province of the keeper's kingdom that concerned the protection of game more than stocking. The river keeper's job was directly concerned with counteracting the poacher and here, even more than on the field or in the wood, the game seemed properly to belong to whoever had the skill or the cunning to catch it. Until the River Boards came on the scene little was done to stock rivers. Salmon and sea trout came upriver to spawn in spring and autumn depending on the length and nature of the particular river—late up the short spate river, and early up the slow, long river. The fish showed at the falls and in lies below bridges. They could be seen in the shallows. Farmers sometimes found them in ditches and got them out with hayforks. They came like the swallow and the cuckoo and only a greedy landlord would have claimed them as his own. He had, it seemed, enclosed land that had belonged to everyone. He sometimes tried to steal the common. He claimed the fish and there were more than he could catch, many more than he could ever eat! The whole thing irked the man who owned nothing. How could a fish that swam up from the sea belong to one man when it didn't belong to another? Did he also own the air? There were old countrymen who would never accept such claims. They were not poaching. They were taking the fish like manna from heaven. If the keeper could stop them he was welcome to try but he might end up in the water and perhaps be drowned. The beauty of catching fish is that it is a quiet business. It can be done by day or by night without advertising the fact. A keeper may walk the banks but he needs to know where to look and there are usually a hundred ways he can be misled. Lines can be set in the bank, nets rigged to intercept the fish or used to draw the pool. A stroke haul, a lump of ironmongery with mutiple hooks, may be used to snag and snatch a salmon from a pool. A man may simply wade in and grab a fish in shallow water or send his dog to bring it for him. He may poison the water with carbide, suffocate the fish with lime, blow them out of the water with explosives or detonators from the quarry, or build a dam to reduce the level of a pool down below so that fish can be reached. Spears are handy tools and the gaff too, with a handle that can be thrown away. The quarry blacksmith makes the snatching hook or the spear. It is easy to use a net and the beauty of this kind of operation is that the gear and the catch can be dropped in the river while the offender argues his innocence. To combat such tactics the river keeper needs to know all the ways and all the places. He also needs to know his man. It is, in fact, impossible to be completely successful against the river poacher and the keeper knows it. What makes the business pay is the ready market, the outlet for the catch. The poacher, unlike the man who trespasses to make a bag of pheasants, may well have a licence to fish, and generally does have one to excuse his presence on the bank during the season. He may be an expert with the fly and a master with the gaff. It takes only a minute to foul-hook a fish and have it on the bank, and no time at all, when it is gaffed, to fix a fly in its jaw to make it look as though it had been legitimately caught. The gangs, of course, aren't out for fish caught one at a time. They come equipped to clear the pool and if necessary fight their way out if they are surprised. The keeper can only contend with them if he is forewarned and has help, and often he has no warning. Salmon tend to run in larger numbers in the days of November and December. The poachers watch the pools and decide where and when they may make the biggest haul. A couple of detonators will stun the fish and leave them floating at the lower end of the pool. Lime or poison takes a little longer to work. The net is less effective unless the pool is free of obstructions but one way or the other the fish are taken and the keeper foiled.

What makes river keeping and poaching different is the extraordinary way the whole thing is regulated. The River Board uses public money to stock the river to provide fish for those who own the riverbank. The stock consists of ova or fry, which, nourished in the stream, migrate as smolts to the sea from which the young fish return to spawn. The landowner owns the river to the middle of the streambed. By this ownership he owns what swims in the water, although he doesn't own the water! The paradox baffles the man who doesn't own the riverbank and incenses him when he is not allowed to fish for fish put there as much at his expense as any other man who pays his rates and taxes. The keeper of the river is as disliked as the keeper of the woods. The law is disliked even more at a time when everyone, rich and poor, wants to fish. In Ireland they have ordered things differently and soon they will have no poaching perhaps, for they plan to cancel riparian right and simply licence the fisherman to use his rod and line.

11

The Shepherd's Place

I T I S difficult to decide where the shepherd belongs in the modern agricultural world. His calling is certainly much older than the business of cultivation. He might tend sheep wherever he found pasture and his sheep were happy to browse wherever they were driven or led, across great plains and over mountain ridges where they encountered only the sailing eagle and the wolf. Like the hungry hunter in pursuit of game, the herd was an explorer. It would be a mistake, however, to suggest that he brought all the sheep and goats domesticated and bred in Europe out of the East. Like the warrior who clawed himself on to the back of the wild horse, he found that the hills and wild mountains were already populated with native wild sheep, and these, it is recorded, interbred with the domesticated animal. The fleeces of these sheep, wild or domesticated, clothed our neolithic ancestors who hunted them and other, larger game, with their stone axes and spears. Ever since this period of pre-history the shape and size of the sheep has been changing.

The neolithic sheep was said to have been more like a goat than our present-day breeds. It probably was and its flesh just as stringy. It needed sinews and fine bones to survive in the fastness of the rocks into which it was driven by hunters. It had become a developed breed of domesticated sheep in Britain by the time the Romans came. They were impressed by the quality of its wool, if not by its meat. They had never seen wool of such fine lustre. Like everything else they found on the frontier of their empire, they sent the wool back to Rome. In England they set up the first wool factory. From this time on sheep began to be of greater importance to the people of Britain until, by the Middle Ages, after Harold had fallen and the Conqueror had brought his weavers from Flanders, wool became the very keystone of the economy. The lustrous wool produced by a climate the Romans had never really taken to, and fostered by the particular herbage our ungentle rains encouraged, was considered so important that its export in a natural state was forbidden. The sheep and the shepherd of the middle ages were as important to the nation as the miner and coal in the present-day energy crisis.

The work of the shepherd has hardly changed at all in thousands of years, but the sheep changed like a chameleon. From being a slender creature with very goatlike horns it grew tall. It became short-legged. It grew a short fleece or a very long one! It was fat and dumpy. It had a Roman nose and flopped ears. It also had fine pointed ears. It had horns and it was hornless. In the process countless breeds of sheep came into fashion to satisfy the wool trade and the butcher. The right sheep for the mountain was one that could live on rough herbage and little else but would produce wool that had the most durable fibres for the hardest-wearing tweed. Such a sheep didn't satisfy the master weaver, however. He wanted lustre wool, warm wool, soft wool. He wanted to make fine woollen cloth and carpets. He wanted the wool of the sheep of the Down and the gentler climate of the Home Counties. He wasn't concerned whether the breed had a Roman nose or a camel's lip, a black face, a brown face, a grey-blue face or a white one. Wool was what he wanted. Charles II had decreed that the dead were to be buried only in woollen shrouds! Wool smuggling was almost as attractive as bringing in French brandy without duty.

On the Downs, the fells, the marshes of Essex and the fens of Norfolk, the shepherd was involved in all this, though he might be almost oblivious to the fact. He tended to be a philosophic fellow. He may once in a while have wondered what the wild mouflon had really looked like. He would have culled it immediately from his flock. It would have looked most odd, even before the fine Leicester breed came along and hundreds of bundly Cheviots bumped their way across the moors along Hadrian's Wall. Sheep breeding has never stopped since the day when wool began to swell the English treasury. Whatever the size and shape, however fine the wool of the present-day sheep, and although it bears no comparison with the ancient turbary sheep, zoologists have a simple definition of the animal. It is a hollow-horned ruminant. It lives in flocks. It is wool-bearing. The scribes marked it down as a sacrificial animal. It has a cloven hoof. They didn't examine the cloven hoof or, if they did, they didn't record the fact that between the toes of this hollow-horned ruminant there is a gland. As the foot splays and the animal moves, this gland secretes a substance that marks the path, leaving an odour which others of the same kind, and perhaps the wolf, can detect. It is a fact that sheep can locate one another by day or by night without seeing each other or even being able to hear the bleating of the flock. They have something like the buttered paws of the old lady's cat who always comes home. It may be that even the shepherd himself, when he began to mind those first few, half-wild sheep, didn't know why his sheep found grass of their own account, sometimes deserting him as he led them over a rise. The message on the track told them that other sheep had gone that way to fill their hungry bellies.

The mere cultivation of sheep to provide us with meat would undoubtedly have left us with very different animals from those to be seen on a journey through Britain today. The spinners and the weavers had as much to do with the sheep's shape and size as anyone. Calling for different fibres, they encouraged the flockmasters in those parts of the country where the wool had the required characteristic. Soft yarns are a delight to the person wearing something woven from them, but soft wool wears badly. The long, ground-sweeping fleece of the Scotch black-face has durable yarn but isn't the ideal choice of the weaver. What weavers needed in the great days before man-made fibres began to take over, were blends of wool. There was no sheep that had every characteristic required and at the same time pleased the butcher and gave every shepherd his living. There was no sheep ideal for Down and fell, able to produce exactly what was wanted on heath, clover and kale. The weather on the bleak northern moor would not have suited the short-wools of the south. The flockmaster held that what made his particular breed of sheep the thing it was disappeared if it was moved, not a couple of hundred miles, but into the next county!

A breeder who recommended one particular breed would have

been laughed at by shepherds looking after scores of other breeds developed and fostered on their own particular terrain. A list of sheep breeds popular in the present century would include the names of the pastoral counties and shires—Leicester, Suffolk, Lincoln and districts too—Cotswold, Wensleydale and Clun. Just as butchers know the butchering breeds, the wool graders know the clip of the best wool breed. They can take a pinch of wool in their fingers and make a shrewd guess as to the place in which the animal was reared. Wool is not simply a material that grows on a sheep's back the way hay rises on a meadow. A layman might hardly credit the difference in its fibre quality. The prime clip is to the wool-grader what a fine wine is to the wine-taster.

The finest wool from a particular sheep is its lamb's wool. The lambswool growth will be shorn when the lamb is about eight months old. A subsequent clip at fourteen months or so is known as hogg wool. The word hogg or hogget is applied to a yearling sheep. All subsequent shearings are called wether wool. The old way of shearing was with hand shears, a pair of blades activated by a broad but not too inflexible spring allowing the shearing action. This was a one-handed operation done while the sheep or lamb was held lightly between the shearer's knees and manipulated by his free hand. In the process of being shorn the lamb would be turned as the hand shears were brought to and fro across its back and down its flanks and belly, leaving slight ridges and a somewhat uneven skin, but bringing the fleece away, whole and unbroken, so that it could be rolled and tied and tossed on to the pile of accumulated fleeces. The business was tiring and time-consuming. Shepherds would get together and work as a group to shear a large flock or flocks, but of course, someone weary of the endless task came to improve on the hand shears, producing a wheel-driven shearer which took some of the tedium out of the business, though it was a question of one man turning a wheel and the other making the device work.

In the very early days the fleeces would be moved by packhorse to a collection centre or local mills where the wool would be scoured, carded and woven into something not much better than homespun although it came from mechanical, power-driven looms. In the north the wool of the Shetlands was used for warm woollen garments, the wool of the black-faces mainly for hard-fibred products and carpets, and the wool of the Cheviot breed for tweeds. It is said that the blood of the Cheviot had a trace of the Merino in it after the Spanish Armada came to grief and some Merinos were washed ashore, but this is a legend which it is doubtful whether anyone could substantiate now.

The wool trade had thriven long before the Leicester breed was produced and its greatest setback was undoubtedly the development of the cotton industry. In the seventeenth century when money meant a great deal more than it does now and the population of Britain was hardly beginning to move towards industry, it was estimated that two million pounds worth of wool resulted in eight million pounds in exported goods. In the eighteenth century a million people were engaged, one way or another, in the wool trade. They depended upon between ten and twelve million head of sheep. At Westminster there were four woolsacks upon which there sat judges and chancellors. Only one of these comfortable seats survives as an emblem of our sometime wool-gathering glory.

The sheep which generations of shepherds have tended must be admitted to be one of the least intelligent of our domesticated animals. It tends to be depicted as a bundle of wool, a leg at each corner with a large-eyed head at the fore-end to balance a clipped tail at the other. In two thousand years the sheep hasn't inspired a single legend depending upon its intelligence. On the contrary its history seems to have pointed in the opposite direction! It could never have wanted its freedom. It had no conception of its destiny even when it saw the knife, poor thing, and its blood ran on the sacrificial altar or over the slaughterhouse floor. It was not perfect. All that was wanted of it was its meat and its wool. The flockmaster made it what it was, accepting in the process that some of the breeds were headstrong if not intelligent. Some refused to sit still and ruminate but wandered like their more nomadic ancestors. This trait was strong in the sheep of the fells and the mountains that were unable to recognize boundary walls and fences. They roamed and the stoutest-hearted fell-runner couldn't always head them off and needed two or three dogs to remain a flockmaster with any sheep to mind. Black-faces would wander and climb walls. Welsh mountain sheep would return to their particular cwm if they were sold off in the market to some incomer.

With all, however, it cannot be denied that the shepherd born of generations of shepherds has always accepted both the stupidity of his flock and the waywardness of some of his sheep. In return the sheep has kept him above the poverty line down through the ages and many a time sheltered with him, sharing their warmth in a blinding blizzard. The good shepherd claims to know the face of every member of his flock. No two sheep are alike, he says. Their faces are as different and as recognizable in their difference as the faces of human beings. When a flock strays the shepherd knows the ram that led them and goes after his strays knowing that they, like the fox that chews on the dead lamb, are only being what they are. A sheep is a sheep and cannot be anything else but what man has made it.

Different breeds of sheep call for a different system of husbandry. The territory makes the breed and the breed must be managed accordingly. Paradoxically a moorland sheep will be fed less than a lowland breed. It manages on a coarser herbage. It can get through winter with little more that a few bales of hay scattered on the lower moor when the snow covers all else, but the lowland sheep will dog the shepherd's heels for a ration in a trough, something more than the bale of hay which the upland sheep is only persuaded to eat in hard times.

The largest breed of sheep inherited by the twentieth-century shepherd was the turnip-eating Lincoln, one of the long-wool breeds. Sheep in general may be listed as long-wools, short-wools and mountain breeds. Most of the smaller, tubby sheep are mutton breeds, prized for their butchering qualities rather than cultivated for their wool. Among the short-wools, and more handsome sheep, some would say, are the Downs which are hornless, dark-legged and fine-woolled. These include South Downs, Suffolk Downs, Hampshire Downs. The short wools have tended to have southern names, being mainly southern breeds from Dorset, Oxfordshire, Wiltshire and Devon. There are of course, flocks of sheep in which the crosses among breeds could only be identified by the expert. As man came from Adam, the family tree of the sheep has innumerable branches!

The long-wools, sheep of pasture, marsh and upland, include the Leicester breed, but once again there are places and localities particularly suited to the land and climate that were cultivated with as much care—Romney and Kent produced Marsh sheep just as distinct in character as those of the Cotswolds, Devon and the Yorkshire Dale or Lincoln. The most important cultivation of a breed was undoubtedly the Leicester produced by a Mr Robert Bakewell. The Border-Leicester, with something of the Cheviot to help the breed along, was the ultimate outcome of Bakewell's contribution to the best breeds of British sheep. The Wensleydales, with their tufted heads and curled fleeces, were considered good stock with which to reinforce the black-face mountain sheep and improve the lamb. The old Cotswold sheep had always held sway in their native counties, a crow flight from the Downs where the sheep of the chalk could be divided into two categories—under-Downs and upper-Downs, the upper-Down being a lighter animal than the breed kept on the lower part of the country. The marsh sheep of the south-eastern part of England were exported to New Zealand, giving the flockmasters of the Antipodes close-coated, long-wools that were short in the leg and thick in the body, a sort of trade-mark for both the butcher and the wool-grower! The South Down sheep is characterized by a small and symmetrical head. It has a brown or fawn face and is fine-boned, while the Hampshire Down, which owes some of its blood to it, has a black face and Roman nose, coming also of old Wiltshire horned stock and the Berkshire sheep. The horned sheep of Norfolk are to be seen in the Suffolk Down, a breed cultivated in the eighteenth century and which has a black face and black legs. The Shropshire sheep of Housman's 'blue remembered hills' was dark-faced and had neat ears. Its blood runs in the Clun. This breed probably saved the Welsh mountain sheep of the early part of this century from disappearing down rabbit holes! The Welsh dwarf had diminished in size. It wasn't the difficulty of sorting sheep from hares that made the poor Welsh flockmaster spend his hard-earned money on the Clun ram, but the demands of the butchering trade. There was no finer lamb in the world than the offspring of the diminutive Welsh sheep, weighing forty pounds or less, but when quantity rather than quality became the rule the little sheep had to be built up to the butcher's standard! There might always be poor shepherds but the rule was that there must never be a butcher who wasn't wealthy!

The hardiest sheep bred in Britain, say the men who attend the northern sheep sales, is the Herdwick. This is probably so, for no sheep lives in a wetter climate than those on the fells of what was once Westmorland and Cumberland.

As long as there are distinct breeds of native sheep there will be experiments to improve on them despite occasional attempts to replace them with novelties from the Mediterranean or the East. The Merino, a white-faced, pink-nosed sheep from Spain, did well in Australia and America, where its quality was improved, before it came again to Britain. Whatever the breed, and however well it does, its care and infant nurture depends, as it always has done, on the work of the shepherd, something very little mechanized beyond the use of mobile shearing equipment and a Landrover to bring the shepherd to his lambing pens. Here, almost as unchanged as the mountain or the downland hogsback, the shepherd must do his work in the twentieth century much as his forefathers have done. He works the flock across the same ground, pens them in the same stone folds or wooden hurdles, and lambs them, late or early, according to the district. In the old days flocks were fed linseed cake, turned on to roots or kale fields, cropped the mountain grazing and finally the valley pastures until they were as threadbare as a worn-out carpet. Medication was a sort of rule of thumb business. Footrot was prevalent. Sheep on over-grazed land advertised their diseased condition and came limping to the pens where they would be upturned and treated with archangel tar. If the agricultural revolution hasn't affected the shepherd's work in many other ways he is now something of a do-it-yourself vet. He can inject his flock for all the diseases sheep are heir to. Liver fluke, once the scourge of sheep on wet grassland, no longer takes such a great toll of the flock brought to green pasture.

It takes between twenty-one and twenty-two weeks to produce a lamb or lambs after the ewe has been served by the ram, and the lambing season is fixed by the time chosen by the flockmaster for the release of rams into the flock. The shepherd doesn't just return the culled rams to the ewes and leave it at that. He would hardly know where he was, come the spring, if he didn't know what had

happened and how well the rams were doing their work. He needs
to be able to tell which ewes have been served and when. This information results from the use of raddle with which the underbelly
of the ram is coloured. Sometimes red is used on the first occasion,
followed by blue and finally black. By examining his ewes the shepherd then knows the interval between the first batch of lambs and
the end of his lambing time. He knows, for instance, whether most
of his labour will be in, say, the last week in March, the middle
of April or later. The gestation period doesn't vary but keeping a
careful watch on the flock and using different coloured 'raddle' is
a guide to what lies ahead. In different parts of the country, because
of the climate, and also in a few special areas, lambing may be
organized early. Lambs can be 'dropped' around Christmas or New
Year's Day and their joints be on the dinner table by Whitsun. The
flockmaster pays a price for the hazard of early lambing and hopes
to get his reward from the money the meat trade is always prepared
to pay for early lamb. Early lambing has been long practised by
the shepherds with large flocks on mild, seaboard slopes, and by
butchers with small flocks bred and tended to provide top quality
lamb. Lamb and mutton were at one time equally sought after by
the gourmet until the meat trade began to 'abolish' mutton. Everything became lamb whether it was teg or wether! The wether is,
in fact, a castrated male sheep, the males being culled and doctored,
generally in early summer, although shepherds with limited lowland
grazing don't often carry them beyond the August lamb sale. Rams
are sold as a rule in September, at the back-end of the shepherd's
year when he is concerned once again with next year's harvest.

Right-hand man to the shepherd is the dog he uses to work his
sheep. Like the wolf with a long line of killers behind him, the sheepdog comes of generations of animals conditioned to stalking without
killing, to shadowing and moving the foolish sheep over ridges,
through defiles and across plains. Like the wolf, this animal works
with others of his kind. The pattern is similar to the wolf pack's
hunting except that the sheep dog has accepted the control of a man.
The shepherd whistles or calls or simply waves an arm and the
dog runs in, drops on its belly, puts its head down on the grass and
watches and waits, glides forward a yard or two, cocks an ear, or
switches its tail from one side of its body to the other. These move-

ments undoubtedly strike some kind of primitive chord in the sheep. The pack is moving in! The sheep stamp their forefeet and jostle one another. Their sides heave, their ears flick and their large eyes bulge. It all happened a thousand years ago when the wolf was everywhere. A good sheepdog doesn't tear a sheep down. It might, a long, long way back in the dim past, have had just a sprinkling of the wolf's blood in its veins, but it is a far different creature from the wolf breed. It is highly intelligent. It hardly needs to be ordered. It works with other dogs, and the man in charge, as part of a team. It is worth a dozen men. The shepherd would not simply be useless at the same job, but would die of heart failure trying to do it! For this reason the shepherd's dog is his most important possession. He is concerned to see it fed. He will rarely ever sell it once he has worked it with his sheep, although he will breed from it and train its offspring and sell them. No one will invent a mechanical sheepdog though he works a lifetime to that end. The shepherd is always in need of two or three dogs because with such a hard life the sheepdog wears out. There is no way it can avoid an early end when it runs itself to skin and bone in the wind and rain, on snow and ice and through great seas of mud. Rheumatism will get it. Its heart will wear out sooner than the heart of a dog that is gently exercised. The shepherd is well aware of this. His best dog has an understudy because there must never come a day when the flock-master is helpless, contemplating a flock on a mountain with no servant to bring it down and herd it through the pens. The dog is never a pet in the same way that a house dog is coddled and looked after, but the bond between the herd and his dog couldn't be closer. If there is telepathy between man and beast it is between the shepherd and his collie. In Britain this animal is invariably a Border or a Welsh collie, almost always black or black and white, thick-coated, broad in the head, light-boned and nimble, weighing much less than the keeper's labrador and running at times almost as fast as a greyhound, though in fits and starts and hardly ever after anything it hasn't been ordered to pursue. The young dog is often trained in tandem with an old one and the old dog will chastise the young one for any dereliction of its duty. Sometimes the shepherd will train his young dog on a long lead, pulling it off its feet when it ignores a command. Sometimes, when he needs to slow it down, he will tie up a foreleg.

Here and there he has been known to forget to untie the leg until too late and the dog becomes a three-legged one.

The shepherd himself might be seen as one of a breed of men contracting out of ordinary society. He is always a self-reliant man and almost always one who follows the trade of his father and grandfather. The elements of his trade are few. His knowledge of sheep and their ways is almost instinctive. He knows where to look for them when they are thornfast. He can tell where they have headed when they are not to be seen on the grazing, and where they will go to shelter in a gale or a snowstorm. He even watches them to know what the weather is going to be, for stupid though they may have been bred, they have some kind of built-in barometer enabling them to take shelter before a storm. Like the fowl of the marsh, or the wintering geese, sheep receive this early warning of change. They come downhill before the rain clouds lower on the mountain. They seek the cover of the gorse and the drystone walls when the yellowing cloud of the snowstorm is far off. The man who tends them is no more a man of the moment than the sheep or the dog with which he herds them. He is a born sheep-keeper and what he knows about them can hardly be appreciated or understood by laymen. The shepherd himself is rarely articulate enough to explain his feelings about sheep or give more than a glimpse of what can only be instinct to anyone making a study of his calling. He marries a woman who must be able to stand a life largely lived in isolation from the village community and the rural population as a whole. His children grow up shy of strangers. His dogs grow to be suspicious of callers. He lives close to his work, close to the grazings, the great expanse of down, the grim heights of the fell, the wild, mist-hugged undulations of the moor, and he meets only men of his own kind.

The machine that opened up the countryside, threshed the corn, brought coals from Newcastle, towed a plough up and down a field, did nothing to change the pattern for the shepherd except when the fleeces were transported, the wool taken from him. The change left him no better dressed, no better fed or housed. He walked the hill with the crook his father carved, as many miles as his grandfather walked. The industrial revolution, which had a great deal to do with looms and weaving, stopped short on the edge of the pastoral wilderness where the wheat and the oats grew. Few other occupations have remained as unaffected by so-called progress. Almost every other trade reaped benefits that made a man's backache less than it had hitherto been. The modern shearer of sheep is usually a contract worker who trims fleeces from two hundred sheep in a day. He is really an extension of the wool industry, the longest tentacle of mechanization the shepherd encounters. There is no other way for the herd, his flock and the wool that grows on its back. It may console this man a little to know that though Hodge may be redundant, and machines roll across vast wheatfields without a minder, this kind of thing will never happen to him. The shepherd's nightmare, if he has one, is that wool itself will be completely replaced by some new fibre spun in a factory, grown out of a vat of cellulose or some kind of gum. When this happens—perhaps when everyone lives in an insulated world of high rise, double-glazed pigeon holes—the dog will be dead and the sheep no longer picking its way on narrow ledges above the scree. The shepherd may be lucky to have his memorial cairn built for him by some compassionate, sentimental lover of things as they used to be.

12

The Man of the Forest

THE INHERITANCE of each new century from that newly gone always seems to be something less and less of a blessing if one looks closely at the background of a nation's history. Once the whole of Britain was a well-forested land with ancient trees; fine oaks, tall elms, great beeches, ash and pine trees of different sorts according to the fertility of the ground. The trees of the chase remained because the population was small and there was more timber than their way of life called for even when it was the principal source of fuel and houses were constructed largely of wood. The economy was agrarian and not very organized. We sold some of our grain and our wool products. Nevertheless we felled trees to build ships. Hearts of oak carried our men in sail right round the world. The man who looked after the woods generally worked harder with the axe than with any kind of cultivating tool. When barns and churches were to be built he looked for trees that would make the longest beams or yield the broadest boards. English brown oak, pickled in cowdung, will last for ever. Hardwood is a long time maturing. It absorbs moisture less readily than softwood after it has been kiln-dried because of its cell structure. Softwood, however, being far less durable, was never a material in which a craftsman cared to invest his labour, particularly in an age when mechanical aids were few. The oak went to the shipyard or into the timbers of the barn. The other highly useful hardwood that would weather well out of doors was the ash. Ash was the choice of the wagon-builder and the maker of carriages. It also, as a sapling tree, provided clog wood, handles for picks and other implements. The magnificent beech, growing out of the floor of the forest like the leg of a mammoth mammoth, was often diseased and its drawback was that it rotted out of doors. Its use was limited to furniture-making (it was the woodturner's favourite) and domestic items of one sort or another.

Time saw to it that the forest clearings increased in area. Nothing that takes as long to grow as a hardwood tree can be replaced in a man's lifetime. But no one seriously gave thought to planting trees—except to harvest them as coppice. The coppice industry, if it could be called that, was a kind of short-term forestry. The land-owner counted his timber as an exploitable asset and stood many an impoverished squire in good stead when the crops failed. It grew like money gathering interest in a bank account, and was converted into sovereigns without delay by selling young trees to the man with a hop field. Withy thickets were cut for the weaver of baskets. A close-grown ash plantation supplied the maker of hurdles. The axe and the saw wrought such devastation in woodlands that it showed. If very little was done to plant trees to replace the old oaks, a forester was always needed to ensure another planting of ash.

Here and there, a far-sighted landowner, concerned not so much for the nation's future needs, but the continued prosperity of his family in generations to come, planted hardwood: but the planting of trees for posterity was beyond consideration. There was no law to say that a man must plant an acorn to replace a tree he cut down. There were already too many regulations controlling the price of corn, the sale of wool, or the employment of children in factories mushrooming in the industrial revolution.

Early in the nineteenth century William Cobbett on his rural rides looked at the conifer trees being planted in different parts of south-ern England and deplored the trend. He was no great authority on forestry himself and probably deliberately disregarded the nature of the land when he deplored investment in softwood which takes not much more than thirty years to mature. He looked at the coppice trade and rode his hobby horse, advertising the false acacia or locust tree, which, he claimed, was an altogether finer timber and a fast-maturing tree. It would be a godsend to the man needing hop poles and it was impervious to all the timber pests he could think of! It took a polish like boxwood. He had seen some very fine furniture made from it in America. He offered locust seedling trees for sale and sold them to more than one important landowner. Had he been right the ash pole would have been discarded. The locust (Robinia) would have taken its place everywhere. Cobbett knew that climate affected the farmer's crops, but he didn't seem to be able to understand that forest trees take much more from the land than a crop of wheat. A good oak can't be grown on scrub land. The deciduous tree draws its moisture from a greater depth than any other growing plant. Its quality is affected by the nutrients in the earth and the water that gives it sap. The locust tree, however fine it might have been in America, proved far short of the ideal tree for England. Its thorny branches seemed to be affected by rheumatism. They were anything but straight. The locust never yielded a good board to the cabinet-maker, or a broad plank to the sawbench. Even the coppice tree was a disappointment. Like the first Merino sheep, brought straight from the sun-baked fields of Spain, the locust underlined the fact that few natives can be transplanted successfully. The oak and the ash had been a long time growing in the damp climate of Britain. The fibres and cells of these woods were really the product of years of sun and rain and temperature variation on a comparatively small island. The tree that needed to be planted was an English tree, the oak, that had provided a thousand ships and ten thousand casks, or the pine that thrived north of the farthest wall the Romans had built to confine the barbarians. It was, oddly enough, in this part of the world, less depleted of its hardwood (not all northern forests are or were of conifer) that the craft and know-how of forestry was developed. One of the reasons for this was that the Scottish estates often had few convertible assets other than their timber. The more frugal Scottish laird didn't need to be reminded that if he cut without replanting, a day would come when he would see the far Cuillins without a tree to block his view! It was the stark reality of the outcome of the use of saw and axe that made a sylvicultrist of a woodman cum forester whose job had largely been felling and supplying logs for his master's fire even if timber had always been the mainstay of an estate's maintenance. Timber was always needed to repair buildings and provide gates and fences for tenants. It was also a valuable raw material when it was sold to contractors supplying the shipyard and the carriage-builders. The output end of estate forestry was revolutionized in the mid 1800's by a sawbench which incorporated a steam engine. Before the steam powered sawmill, timber felling had been a slow and laborious business. Horses or oxen would drag the dressed trunk from the wood to the sawing pit where the work was done with crosscut saws. Men would spend days stripping bark with an adze, cutting the tree into rough boards or shaping the log so that it might serve as a roof tree when oxen hauled it away on a limber. The steam engine changed the slow preparation of felled timber for the market, but by the very nature of the forest it was prevented from going in and bringing the tree to the sawbench. This remained work for the ox and the workhorse to do. The horse was generally preferred because it was a more nimble creature, even though it might lack the brute strength of the great ox. The forester whose job it was to raise trees could look for very little in the way of equipment to make his task lighter. There wasn't even a plough to drain moorland for replanting. Everything had to be done the hard way. The forester began where every gardener begins, in the nursery, where he raised seedlings. Although trees he had left standing occasionally blessed him with naturally generated seedlings he could never rely on these. Stool growth of cut trees was not a very good proposition. He had to plant his acorns with a multiple dibber, dropping an acorn into each hole, and trusting that the crow or a squirrel wouldn't unearth the seed! He had to wait a very long time for the result in the case of hardwood trees and planted faster-growing softwoods between his rows, like a gardener catch-cropping. Even when he cleared ground he was at a disadvantage with the plant life already germinating in the rich compost of what had once been woodland. Growth that developed too fast suffocated the seedling, although occasionally young trees would benefit from early shelter. Even so, where gorse and heath sprang up the young tree was deprived of both light and nourishment. The nineteenth century forester didn't have to go to college to learn ecology. He was taught bitter lessons on the ground, year by year, and his master looked for forests of hardwood or conifer as he looked for a stag on every hillside and grouse on the moor!

The conifer tree was a delight to the men at the sawbench. It rolled easily. It ran through the saw guides, throwing up sawdust as the steam train threw out redhot coal. The world was crying out for timber of any sort as the years rolled past. The steam-engined boat made of iron was in the minds of men like Brunel, but wooden clippers still raced across the Atlantic to get back from America before winter. Wooden crates, wooden casks, wood for the wagons that brought up the rear when Wellington prepared to meet Napoleon, wood for rifles—and wood for stretchers by the time it was all over. The day of the forester really arrived when the day of the great forests was at an end. If poor men had been buried in woollen shrouds, their more fortunate and more important brothers were buried in elm—and figured oak. The railway trundled in to take timber away. Even rolling stock depended upon durable wooden wagons.

There never would be enough timber in the world, least of all in a country that had no thought for tomorrow. People who had given up burning wood for coal and coalgas looked at pictures by masters—leafy scenes painted by Constable and Turner—and imagined that trees were always there, the way rain was in the clouds!

The forester came out of the nineteenth and into the twentieth century largely unrecognized. People were too fascinated by the distance they could now travel—the speed at which locomotives could eat up the ground between London and Oban or Inverness—to think that anyone cultivated trees. No one had actually planted our forests, however tidily they were kept behind fences and perimeter hedges! They were there because Rufus had hunted. They were there because Charles had hidden in an oak. By chance a stout oak tree made furniture and an ash furnished timber for a brougham or a railway wagon. There were bigger and better forests in Germany. People who had travelled that far said that Finland was nothing but one great forest. The endless tracts of spruce and pine supplied white and red deal for cheap furniture and the woodwork of miners' houses that stood in terrace rows.

The steam engine of the sawmills worked overtime. The forester and his team of tree-planters were rather like men on foot trying to keep up with the London to Edinburgh express. People who knew about trees and the management of woodland were few in number. There were books on how to smelt iron, how to keep an internal combustion engine running, or a telegraph office working, but very few books of any kind on sylviculture. Those who consumed the timber thought no more about its source than those who threw coal on the fire were concerned about how much of it might lie under ground.

The Great War, when it came, devastated more than battle fields. It harvested and used timber faster than any other process of destruction man could have devised unless he had made a bonfire. Softwood was at a premium. Woods everywhere were put to the saw and the axe and great deserts of treestumps quickly hidden in foxgloves, ragwort and nettles. The wilderness had come into its own with a vengeance. It was obvious at last that large-scale forestry would have to be undertaken to reclothe the hills, forestall erosion and, above all, provide the timber a surviving generation would need. There was a world shortage of timber. In Britain the government blessed the setting up of what was to become the Forestry Commission. The Treasury granted loans. They were repayable with interest, of course, though the timber itself might have been thought a rich enough reward for a people who had been so extravagant with natural resources. The tree-planters set to work on a scale that was modest enough considering what needed doing.

Britain's nucleus of forestry skill when horsepower became brake horsepower and agriculture became mechanized, derived entirely from private estates and its few Crown forests. The subject was barely defined as any sort of science. It was something for academics to specialize in and the man from the wood to work at. It would have been difficult for either of them working in the field to say whether he was properly called a tradesman or aspired to a profession. The man who has a skill can demonstrate it and the practical woodman, the old forester who had hardly read a book, could, given time, demonstrate his skill and apply his practical experience. The academic knew why the peat bed wouldn't support plant life and could assess the chemical deficiency of the land, but he wasn't a practical tree-planter and perhaps he borrowed the old forester's good name. The forester's calling, like that of the shepherd and the gamekeeper, was one in which a man found himself often by force of circumstance. He was a forester because his father had worked in the woods. It was the only trade to which his family could think to put him. It was as natural for the youngster to go into the woods as for the miner's son to follow his father into the coalmine. No one pretended that it was a soft life in the woods, with birds singing and the breeze rustling the leaves. It was very far from that. The young apprentice walked as many miles as the shepherd and worked harder, day in and day out, than the keeper, developing in the process an instinct for the cultivation of trees. An acre of land planted with grain or potatoes may be prepared with a plough and a harrow, sown in a few days or planted as fast as a man can walk up and down the furrows. The forester, although he didn't plough the land, invariably had to clear it. The planting might not be done as a gardener plants a fruit tree but involved, and still involves, a great deal of backache. There never would be an easy way. The business would always be as basic and elemental as keeping sheep on the moor. No machine man could devise would plant a hillside and change it into a forest.

There are two categories of forestry that call for different techniques of cultivation and plantation management: the establishment of deciduous woods and the growing of conifers. In places these may overlap or intermingle to a certain degree. One is short-term forestry in that the life of a pine tree may be something like eighty to a hundred years, though it may mature much earlier, and the other is hardwood planting, generally done on a much more modest scale and often, it must be said, with an eye to landscape and amenity in the future rather than with intention to reap a financial benefit in less than a century. A forester might or might not be given the authority to plant the tree of his choice, but his advice on the species of tree would be sought by an intelligent employer seeking to make a wood of hitherto virgin land. The forester's instinct would be conservative. He would have seen how the pines he planted as a boy on the fringe of the moor dwarfed as they grew or went over in the gale, and how the sitka, for instance, flourished. He would have been taught how to raise his nursery trees and when to transplant. He would know the quality of the seed he needed to gather and the best place to get it. He would also know when and where to interplant one species of tree with another to provide each with a certain shelter or shade at a critical stage in its growth. Conifer planting might seem to the layman the regimentation of firs and pines in blocks, but the fact is that certain species of tree do well on particular ground and others do not. Some dwarf near the tree-line. Some must have nutrients which they can barely get on light and shallow loam. A great many pines will fall in a wind if they have been planted without thought for their characteristic root structure. It may be fatal to fell a section of them when they mature, if they have been planted in the wrong place, because the wind will run through a funnel and uproot hundreds more that will only be extracted with great difficulty when many of them are interlocked and badly damaged. This kind of know-how was the forester's inheritance, the almost taken-for-granted knowledge acquired by his elders and passed on as something commonplace and not at all remarkable. It would save time in fifty years. It would ensure timber of the right size and quality. Looking at the conifer blocks few laymen would ever appreciate that the work had been done with serious deliberation to create a forest, rather than a background, but a source of wealth and something vital to the economy rather than picture-book landscape. A forest is a lot of trees. It is also land that has been cleared and drained. The old forester had no crawling drain ploughs as big as a dinosaur, no mechanical grubbers to tear out the scrub and the rhyzomes of bracken. He had to dig his peat drains the hard way, with the draining shovel, and peat is as heavy to dig as the claybed. Forestry work is probably as much about land drainage as anything else, for it is essential to halt erosion, to keep the watershed from washing the shallow upland soil from the rocks to silt the streams and the rivers lower down. The root structure of a thousand trees acts as a barrier to the flow of water downhill. The forester channels the excess in his peat drains which feed the streams. His trees hold the soil and prevent its erosion not only by flood, but ultimately by the wind. The plan for planting makes it necessary to establish blocks of close-growing young trees. The forester knows how far apart different kinds of young trees are best planted. They have to be repeatedly thinned out as they grow. In the early stages the proximity of one nursery tree to another will discourage the natural growth which the soil generates but the ground will also have to be kept clear of weeds and creeping thorns of one sort or another—bramble and dogrose, or the seeded gorse that once clothed the area. Thinned trees bring a return from poles used in rustic work, Christmas trees perhaps, fence posts, and finally pit props. The mature tree will ultimately go for paper pulp.

Plodding to his work on the hill, the forester will carry his midday meal in his knapsack and his planting tools and young seedlings in a sack over his back. He will do this kind of work in the cold months of the year, in November and later in the winter so long as there is no danger of young trees being killed by frost. He will plant his trees in rows, turning a measuring stick end-over-end to establish the distance apart of each tree he puts in. The planting may be done in several different ways. One of these is simply 'spading' the young tree into the cut turf and heeling the turf firmly upon it. Another way is the use of the dibber which makes a hole in which the tree is placed. The dibber is then used to lever the soil tightly against the planted tree. A more effective way is the cutting and over-turning of the sod through which the young tree is inserted so that its root structure may develop and benefit from the rotting down of the turf. Whatever method the forester may use, there is no easy way. Perhaps his only consolation is that if it takes a long time to plant a forest, once it is established his work is a little less arduous and exacting.

Forestry entails much more than the planting and thinning of the trees, however. Invariably the forester has his natural enemies. Some of these are the very things the keeper and the shepherd cultivate. Deer browse on young conifers and 'bark' deciduous trees. Sheep must be fenced out because a herbivore is a herbivore and a hungry sheep will devastate a plantation of young trees if it can get at them. The black grouse will eat the tips of the fir. The squirrel, the native red squirrel, now a rare creature in most forests, was one of the great enemies of the old forester who took great satisfaction in contriving their destruction. The rabbit and the hare had no taste for the bark of the pine and were tolerated in conifer areas to some extent, but where there were deciduous trees they would kill them off by ringing the bark, cutting it from the trunk with their chisel-like teeth until the tree died. The forester had to become an expert in fencing things out from his plantations, constructing barriers high enough to discourage a stag that could jump hedges taller than a man, and burying wire netting to exclude the burrowing rabbit. Inside the boundary he had to snare and trap or shoot the predators he had inadvertently confined. He was farming his land as much as a man who planted oats or wheat. The only difference was that he might be cultivating thousands of acres and waiting a whole life-time for the harvest! Every old forester was aware that he could never see the outcome of his labour. A middle-aged man who planted a Norway spruce could hardly expect to see more than thinnings or pit props. He would never see his trees go through the mill and study the grain of boards to discover how they had grown on a par-ticular slope of the hill, or what checks hard winters had inflicted on the growth of the trees.

Before attention was closely focused on the production of trees for the timber industry, and softwoods in particular, the forester concerned with deciduous woods might need to know how to manage the natural regeneration of his trees—re-establishing wood-land other than by replanting. Hardwoods do not take kindly to being uprooted and the transplanting which actually improves the conifer's roots. This natural replacement could be managed by first of all cutting down close canopied trees to improve the humification of the ground beneath, followed by the felling of 'seeding' trees which had benefited by having more light and the warmth of the sun to improve their seed. To ensure the germination of the seed and the growth of seedlings in oak and beech woods, the grazing of pigs, for instance, something commonly done in the larger oak and beech woods of the southern parts of Britain, would be prohib-ited. The observant woodman would take note of the thick flower buds occurring every seven to ten years and fell accordingly in the following winter. The felling itself and the extraction of the tree-trunks would often do the same work as cultivator and harrows did on the arable fields for the farmer. The complete felling of trees in a wood selected for regeneration would never be carried out in one or even two seasons, because the regenerating seed as it de-veloped would need protection not only from the forest, but the heat of the sun which might otherwise have scorched its tender shoots. Even in pine forests regeneration might be adopted by a similar method, the trees being felled at intervals of two to three years, leaving perhaps twenty or thirty to the acre. In this case sheep might be brought in to crop back heather and pigs allowed to root in the bracken, the pine seed not being an item the pig would forage for. As soon as the animals had served this initial purpose, and before the seedlings sprouted, the grazing area would be fenced off and a crop of young pines would flourish in due course. With all his skill in tree-planting the forester would favour the tree grown where the seed fell.

In the main and by force of circumstance, forestry and the forester's work in the twentieth century has become subservient to the consumer in a way incomparable with anything that had taken place in previous centuries. The production of pitprops and railway sleepers was once the standby and generally the principal support of forestry. But the steam train has gone. Railway mileage has contracted and track-laying has become prefabrication. Coal mines need less timber. The output of the forest goes mainly for wood pulp. The lime tree, the poplar and the aspen might give a white and altogether finer pulp, but there never were enough trees of this kind to meet the demand. They couldn't be grown where the spruce flourishes. The spruce yields a yellow pulp obtained by grinding or milling its woody fibre. Conifer woods yield vast quantities of pulping timber roughly six to eight inches in diameter and six or seven feet in length. Barked and cut into suitable lengths for grinding, the spruce wood is forced against a fine-grained sandstone under a continuous stream of water to make the fibres separate, after which they are strained, dried and prepared for use in the manufacture of paper and cardboard. The forester working with the axe and saw was never greatly concerned with what finally happened to his trees. Like the keeper, his job is producing the living thing. If there is any special satisfaction at the felling of the tree it is generally at the quality of the timber and the thought of how the ground may finally be replanted.

One of the hazards of felling a conifer wood, a pine wood in particular (pine is not the woodpulp tree because of its high resin content) is the infestation of tree stumps by the pine weevil, one of the most destructive pests in plantations of pine, spruce, larch and fir in their stages of growth up to five or six years of age. To contend with the threat of this pest a forester has to grub out his tree stumps, fire the ground, or set about barking every stump left on the area. As an apprentice the old forester might have been set to trap and handpick beetles lured to resin-coated bark or bundles of newly-lopped pine branches spread on ground sheets.

The pests of the forest, apart from destructive animals and birds, are mainly its parasitic insects. The maybug or cockchafer feeds on the flowers of the oak, defoliates the tree and is almost as fond of the small green tufts of the sprouting larch and the flowers of the pine. As a grub it lives in the soil. It voraciously attacks the roots of plants and seedling trees, hibernating in three seasons to pupate in June and emerge as a beetle in May of the following year. Cursing the roosting starling, the old forester would nevertheless put up nesting boxes to encourage them, for he could rely on these industrious, insectivorous birds to eat as many maybugs or maybug grubs as they would uncover. Despite the fact that he may fell trees with a petrol-driven chain saw the forester lives the same life and practises the same skill that was handed down to him by the old woodman. Here and there they bring a woodpulp pipeline nearer to the forest and give him a crane or tree-extracting equipment more in keeping with modern mechanical development but he still plants and cultivates trees as he has always done.

13

The Hunting Field

LANDOWNERS AND SQUIRES of the seventeenth and eighteenth centuries were so obsessed with hunting that many of them undoubtedly wasted their substance and came to near ruin in pursuit of the fox. Kings in their day had suffered from a preoccupation with things connected with the chase, but foxhunting was something different. To begin with, the fox had been barely admissible as an animal of the chase but when it was elevated to respectability it ultimately became part of a romantic picture cherished by many people living outside the rural scene, and this persists. The basic inspiration may be a picture of rolling parkland with gorse covers, warm looking red-bricked farmsteads sheltered by their own rookeries, or whitewashed huddles of steadings on the lower slopes of fells. Men and women who people this landscape scatter corn for hens, lean on gates or drive the plough, while the hunt, resplendent in scarlet coats, rushes at the gallop after the fox. Foxhunting is either as traditional to the English mind as that stage-coach Christmas dream, or is regarded as one of the horrors perpetrated by red-faced hunting men and their eagle-beaked women filling in their useless lives. Somewhere between the two the hunting man canters along, not greatly concerned about his image, neither a villain nor a saint, cherishing no hope of persuading the anthropomorphic townsman that what he sees is coloured not by scarlet coats and blood so much as by his own emotion.

It depends how far the researcher cares to look for the origins of hunting. Hunting, as every schoolboy knows, was the full-time occupation of our cavemen ancestors for hunting man had to hunt to live. Kings hunted to enjoy themselves but the savage had to face the boar or the stag at bay with a spear. He had little else to assist him at the kill but the curs he kept. Perhaps it was the very fact that deer, boar and even badger could be eaten, while a fox was a kind of carrion, that prevented the fox from being considered a respectable form of venery when kings hunted. In the chase royal hunters didn't bother with the fox. It tended to go to ground, as indeed the badger did, but since it couldn't be eaten it was left for the attention of those menials responsible for attending to vermin. No man who was part of the king's hunting entourage would have stopped to hunt rats.

There were all sorts of hunting dogs, greyhounds, wolfhounds, deerhounds and small dogs for getting at animals that went below ground. The foxhound wasn't thought of until someone who must have been more a lover of the chase than his contemporaries discovered the most important characteristic of a fox. The fox has a strong odour and one that is quite unmistakable on a still day. This is not, however, a heavy scent. It is soon dispelled by the breeze. It never really marks the trail as does the heavy scent of the stag. It is therefore something very special—the best kind of hunting scent, one belonging to an animal fast on its feet, resourceful and equipped with most remarkable hearing. The true-bred hound is hypnotized by fox scent. It holds him like aniseed. The layman might think that the balance is weighted against the fox once the hound is on his scent for all that seems to happen then is that the pack runs the fox into the ground while the hunters gallop madly behind blowing horns. The truth is that the whole pack must be cast and hunted by a skilled huntsman, for the fox is a survivor.

There was a time in some parts of the country when foxes were hard to come by and enthusiasts would import French and German foxes in order to hunt these miserable transported creatures. A bag fox—one caught in another parish and released the night before the hunt—could be supplied by fox poachers. Gamekeepers were often anxious to get rid of foxes in their own preserves. The local animal, running its own familiar countryside, carries a map in its head. He also has the experience of being hunted there. Contrary to popular belief, there is very little desperation in any move the fox makes when he runs from the gorse kennel or the shelter of some thicket. He is not in panic. The pack must find ways to bundle through hedges and fences. The fox has those familiar runs. He may race across the open pasture with his brush rippling, but a few minutes later he will trot unconcernedly with hounds only a field away, the horn sounding and babblers babbling while whips discourage skirters and inexperienced young hounds from fussing over useless scent. The hunted fox will actually pause and look over his shoulder before he picks his way along the ditch or slips through a hole in the wall. His ears bring him the sound of creaking leather, the snorts of excited horses, the heavy breathing of riders jogging to find a way round some obstacle too formidable to jump. There is probably no native animal better equipped to survive than the fox. The wolf, exterminated and long afterwards reviled, had always been a much greater menace to the verderers and keepers of flocks. The wolf was a pack-hunting animal while the fox is more an individualist!

Hunting men called the fox by different names. He was Reynard here and Charley there. In Wales he was simply Cadno. He lived and thrived because he was almost omnivorous. He could get along without chicken or goose for he could take mice and rats, rabbits, hares, game of any kind and might even get by on beetles and insignificant titbits. He would chew on the ribs of dead sheep, clear up the remains of the sickly lamb or feed on the midden refuse. Had he been an animal large enough to kill a full-grown sheep or bullock he would have gone from the scene, driven into the open and killed by fire and shot, destroyed in his earth by dogs or poison. He had no more than a delinquent record however. He had never flanked a solitary man in a snow storm, driving him out of his mind with fear of the pack. He had never been accused of taking a baby from its cot. He was less of a menace than rats in the granary and he had the blessing of the squires! When country gentlemen found the cockpit too noisy and they wagered too often foxhunting was a popular diversion. It began to flourish with some semblance of organization in hound and horse-breeding in the seventeenth century. Its real hey-day, however, the golden years as some would call them, came in the early nineteenth century when every countryman who could sit a horse and hire a hack turned out to follow hounds. There were famous packs from the eighteenth century—Belvoir, Badmington, Brocklesby and Milton. A changing pattern resulting from the industrial revolution later on brought subscription packs when even the wealthiest landowner could no longer support the high cost of a proprietary hunt. Ultimately there would be (in the 1970's) as many as 400 hunting packs.

The elements of foxhunting remain the same as ever—the fox, the foxhound and man, mounted or on foot. The hunting man bred the hound. There never really was a shortage of foxes and the importing of mangy animals from the Continent didn't last for long. The bag fox was no substitute for the local fox because it was generally disorientated and really didn't perform well. It was coincidental that foxhunting became more popular around the turn of the eighteenth century when land was being fenced or walled as a result of the land enclosure acts. Barbed wire immediately became a great curse to those who had always galloped freely across the shires. Railways were cursed too, but the huntsman detested canals even more for even the boldest rider couldn't clear them, while both hounds and fox could swim across them and often did. There was another curse on foxhunting. The pheasant covert was guarded by those who had no time for foxhunting. A private war was often waged. Keepers poisoned foxes. Farmers dug them out in revenge for damage the hunt did to growing crops or the fox's invasion of the poultry run. There were hunting people who said the keeping of cattle spoiled the scent and the railway too, with its treated wooden sleepers interfered with the pack after the fox. It is a fact that a fox's odour is masked by creosote. The world wasn't going quite as the autocratic landowner or squire might have liked and it was costing as much as £5000 per annum to keep a respectable pack in the Home Counties! The subscription pack produced a committee and the committee paid the bills. It contributed to the upkeep of hounds where once the old squire's tenants had to feed a hound or even forfeit a lease. The committee were inclined to take over and the Master could find himself being told where the pack should be entered at the beginning of the day. He was often glad to delegate the management of hounds to a professional huntsman. It was nevertheless a colourful world. It always had been. The scarlet coat (called pink later on in the nineteenth century) came into fashion. Masters superbly mounted might keep their place at the head of the field by using second and third horses strategically placed along the way.

Literary men recorded the exciting events of the day. Subalterns and their captains rode to hounds. An officer in a fashionable regiment kept at least one hunter. Gentlemen poured themselves into tight breeches and rode on short stirrups with their buttocks bobbing beneath their coats. Ladies sat side-saddle and wore veiled tophats. The field bedazzled the peasantry.

Those who took no active part in the hunt stood on the fringes of the meet to recognize and be recognized by the squire and his son, the parson, his lordship's agent, the country lawyer, the successful merchant and everyone who was anyone for miles around. When the pack moved to the crack of whips and the yelping of hounds impatient to be cast, foot-followers joined the stampede and were jostled on to verges or showered with clods of turf by riders anxious not to be left too far behind. The foot-followers loved to see the Master and his servants bobbing out there ahead of the field and watched eagerly when hounds were entered. In the dead and sagging bracken they might come upon the first tell-tale odour of a lying-out fox whose earth had been stopped the night before. This scent was as tantalizing to hounds as a whiff of roast pheasant from the timbered inn. The sound of the huntsman's horn was echoing magic. Who didn't smile, knowing the fox was under no stress when he so obviously didn't take pursuit seriously? Even when he ran for his life who was there among the gate-openers and forelock-touching labourers who hadn't known some personal disaster when that same fox, or one very like him, had discovered capons being fattened for Christmas or the goose for Michaelmas? The whole rural population, in scarlet, ratcatcher or earth-stained, strapped moleskins, were foxhunters to a man. The true countryman could never be anything else! Rich or poor, they sailed over the wire or cursed it, splashed through gutters and sometimes came to grief—in mind and spirit, if not in body. They all knew an accelerating heartbeat at the far-off view halloo. If the hunt brought a labourer no more than a sixpence for opening a gate or holding a horse, it brought wonderful colour to life.

As with everything man does to create his own entertainment or sport, rules and ritual were built round hunting, otherwise it might have degenerated into a wild orgy of careering after disorientated hounds continually changing foxes. The rules were formulated by the Masters for the proper management of the pack and the hunting field. A social ritual was inescapable when a great many people took to the field to be seen and to enjoy, not so much the hunt, as the exhilaration of riding headlong across open country in the fresh, clean air. Regulating the behaviour of the field was essential because hunting is a craft. The novice might not be aware of the fact that casting a pack of hounds calls for a flair for hunting. The professional huntsman knows every hound not just by its marks and its physical characteristics, but by its voice. He has walked it as a pup in the company of other hound pups. He has exercised it and entered it to cub-hunting and taught it the name of the game. His success depends upon this intimate knowledge of the hound, its blood and its background. An obsession with hounds and hound-breeding were always at the very root of foxhunting. The most highly-prized huntsman serving under a Master was always a man not simply born to the business, but with several professional huntsmen, kennelmen or huntservants in his family tree. Today his ways with the pack and his success in finding a fox earn him the admiration of both the Committee and the field. Traditionally he added to his salary by passing the hat at the kill. No one begrudged him his just reward. While such a professional may bask in the admiration of the field he is critical of wayward members. He is cast down if he loses his fox and his judgement is proved wrong. He has no patience with an over-talkative hound. A hound that turns after a hare drives him into a fit of anger. He relies on his leaders to find 'that which was lost'. When he hears a leader speak he may gauge how far ahead the fox is. But he really doesn't expect a medal for finding his fox. He may present the brush to someone who has done particularly well with the Master's blessing. His job is to think like both fox and hound, the real talent of all huntsmen. This is a thing even the huntsman himself couldn't explain but is something possessed by very few. The ordinary hunt member is also familiar with the voices of hounds and will look hopefully to see a fox put out where one was started before, but the old huntsman knows what his favourites are saying and discounts the clamour of the foolish and excitable ones. A fool always speaks oftener and has less to say! A young hound would back-track a scent were it not for the leaders. But the leaders save their breath to cover ground and their voices are music to the huntsman. Without such animals there might well be no hunt. The most dedicated foxhunters would have to hack home, mud-bespattered and dejected, following in the steps of those who gave up at the first major obstacle.

Hunt servants perform all the tasks that lead to the success of the hunt. They may be kennelmen, responsible for the health and well-being of the pack, whippers-in or whips who support the huntsman in controlling the pack, or youngsters with the craft to learn, who groom and exercise animals and wait upon the Master. At the top of the tree the professional huntsman may become a legendary figure. His reputation spreads because the hunting fraternity talk of him in other counties. He can find another place without being out of work. He lives for horses and hounds and from his youth has been fascinated by the paraphernalia of the kennel and the stable, charmed by the horn. He thinks no more about the kill than he does about the chase that leads to it. This is his trade and like the keeper he can never be involved with the quarry. The job undoubtedly grew out of the landowner's need for a man to look after his hunting dogs, hounds, spaniels and such animals as he used in pursuit of deer, otter and hare. The foxhound it has been said, has a bloodline that goes back to antiquity and this is true of course. It is a pack-hunting animal. It has a highly-developed nose. Some of its ancestors hunted the deer. Its bone and its nose suggest the bloodhound as well as the little basset, but the tree has many roots and as much care and study has gone into the bloodline of the hound as that of the racehorse or the prize bull. The French did more for hound blood than most but the English nobility played their part in giving the fox hunter the foxhound. Like the pheasant driven over guns the product can't really be properly identified as to origin. There is often talk of the Southern Hound, an animal as mystical, it would seem, as the great Black Horse, but there are other blood donors, a trace of colour, a tinge of woad in which some people see wild Britons fighting Romans with hounds snarling in support. There is of course, a native rough-coated hound that seems to belong on the Welsh hills and rivers where the otter is hunted. Bassets and beagles have been bred up or down. The 'recipes' go back beyond pedigrees and the hunting hound would be much less fascinating were this not the case.

There are three forms of hunting other than foxhunting that still flourish today. Two of them are on the decline and all of them go back farther in the history of hunting than the pursuit of old Charley. Deer were hunted with a variety of deerhounds until recently when they began to be hunted with foxhounds. The technique of deer hunting is entirely different from foxhunting because deer herd together. Only very occasionally will a deer run directly away from other members of the group. For herding animals there is a natural instinct to converge on one another. A selected victim hunted by a pack can escape and survive. To ensure that the energies of the pack, and the time of the huntsman, were not wasted chasing deer at random it was necessary to hunt a 'tufter', a hound specially selected to mark the quarry and then diverted and separated from the pack to enable the chase to continue. Deer hunting declines now because the quarry is harder to find in the sort of country over which it might be hunted. It was in ancient times a beast of the hunting chase and the chase is no more. The carted stag, like the bag fox, is no longer considered a worthy quarry.

When it comes to minor hunting and the quarry of those devoted to such small game as the hare, there is a choice of hound—beagle or basset. The hare is hunted both on foot and on horseback with harriers. The beagle could be called a half-pint hound. It is trained as a pup to a drag in which an aniseed rag or a bone is used. When full-grown it appears on the field no more than fifteen inches high. If these small hounds make a run of four miles it is a very long one, but their short legs probably move as many times in this distance as those of a foxhound on a fourteen mile point. The hare makes a hunt with beagle, basset or harrier a strictly parochial affair because the hare tends to keep within his familiar country and run in a circle. In spite of his March madness and his occasional erratic behaviour when competing with visiting jacks for the favours of females, he is no fool. He sits tight for as long as he dares while a feathering pack of small hounds busies itself in dead grass. He slips away with his ears down, running low on the open field, taking cover in the tunnels of swedes or the forest of kale. Bustling beagles will soon be after him if the whips spot him sneaking away. When he bobs over the wall he will run through the sheep and leave the area in their company by a gateway. He has long known that his scent is lost in the reek of sheep and small hounds are foiled. It sometimes happens that the pack turns out another hare in the same rootfield and old countrymen solemnly swear that this is a hare strategem. Hares, they insist, take over from one another! The little beagles are followed on foot and the hunt is enlivened by the twists and turns of the hurrying hare. The basset is a bigger animal, altogether much more powerful. The breed was introduced from France in the latter part of the nineteenth century and increased in popularity with the passing of time. A hound for every quarry, the old hunting man said, and the basset probably seemed more like a hound to men who took time out from foxhunting. It weighs between 40 and 50 lb. It is barrel-bodied, long and low rather than tall, but with a suggestion of the old bloodhound's head, long ears and deep chest. Foot-hunting the hare is a business for a man who loves to be close to things. Scent is invisible and fleet hounds put distance between themselves and less able riders or those on inferior mounts. The foothunter goes as far and as fast as his legs may carry him. In fell hunting the fox hunter needs to be a kind of a John Peel and generally must be content with distant views. Hunting the hare he scrambles and runs to keep up and the Master relies upon him to act as whip if the occasion arises.

The otter, like the hare, has a long history as the quarry of hounds. More than seven hundred years ago otter-hunting was the sport of kings. The office of otter-hunter was a royal appointment in Queen Elizabeth's day and her majesty had her own pack of otter hounds. What attracted the hunter to the otter was the same sort of thing that later brought the fox to his attention—the nature of the scent. The otter is a member of the mustilidae. It has a musky odour. There is nowhere a scent hangs longer than in a riverbed with banks of gravel or silt across which the otter has trailed his low-slung body, but to add to the attractiveness of a good scent is the factor that the otter doesn't leave that scent everywhere. He may submerge and swim a long way, escaping underground or into some tributary or feeder of the river, and his elusiveness becomes quite baffling when there is a wind. Until pollution affected so many of our rivers the otter proved itself well-equipped to survive. It might be cursed by those who used nets and wanted the salmon but it didn't do great harm to the stock of fish. It lived on frogs and eels, small mammals as well as fish. It was often encountered well away from the river in ditches and narrow waters in which there were no fish except eels or crayfish. It sported itself along the bank. It bred up and had its seasons. It was always reported scarce in one decade and plentiful in another, and it was the perfect quarry for the leisurely hunt with hounds that took to water because it bred in winter and was hunted in summer. Otterhounds, enthusiasts would claim, have a scenting capacity exceeding that of all other breeds of hound and they must have more, for the perfect otter hound needs more. The scent of the otter may linger in places for as much as twelve hours but the otterhound separates the old scent from the fresh one. The summer hound is for the most part rough-coated. Occasionally there may be one or two foxhounds in a pack but the traditional hound is in no way a draft from a foxhunter's kennel. Crossbred hounds may fail. The otterhound is bred to hunt the otter and wastes no time with skulking moorhens or hares in adjoining meadows. It can swim at a vigorous dog-paddle just about as fast as the otter can swim underwater. Swimming hounds will trail away in the swiftly flowing current of the river but come up again on the far bank to check the scent in the tree roots. When the otter runs the bank it arches its back and bounds along as though activated by some kind of spring. When it goes below it may have to be bolted by a wiry, rough-coated little terrier brought along for the purpose. A kill is far from inevitable because the otter is in his natural element. He almost always has two or three exits by which he can regain the water. In ancient times, however, the otter hunt was a bloody buiness. Hounds or dogs were not the force as much as men with nets, spears, rakes and poles. The grain, a two-pronged spear, was the favourite weapon until such barbarities were proscribed by a more humane otter-hunting fraternity. What evolved as otter-hunting was a strangely leisurely dalliance along the river. According to authorities on the subject the smoking of clay pipes epitomized the proper attitude of the otter-hunter. Blank days undoubtedly became more frequent when the method changed but the otter had never been easy to kill even with nets and spears. Early in the nineteenth century however, otter-hunting was found to be in a decline.

Otters were scarce on English rivers although they were more than plentiful in Scotland. The strongest opponents of otter-hunting lacked influence until the effects of pollution showed quite plainly that the otter was threatened. Alarm drowned the hunter's horn which barely sounds now. Conservationists and anti-blood sport movements put the otter hunt beyond the pale.

Opposition to hunting has from the beginning not only emphasized the hopelessness of the townsman and the countryman ever seeing the other's point of view, it has been coloured by political leanings and snobbery. The peasant couldn't join in when few of them had mounts but even riders in ratcatcher were discouraged. The hunt was a social occasion and everyone in the community either knew their proper place or were soon enlightened. Farmers in 'pink' were looked on with amusement. The hunting field was for the squire and his accepted equals, his privileged friends. No one in the country was greatly irked by the social distinction but the townsman saw in the hunting field not a little of the arrogance of the millowner, the ironmaster, the coalowner. The image of the Master of foxhounds towered head and shoulders above servile peasants and lackeys. What more useless pastime could there be than one involving a collection of quaintly dressed people with nothing to do, rushing over the fields after a wretched fox? The blooding of the young entrant was a barbarity. The whole business was symbolic of feudalism, the hand of the landowner holding a whip over the miserable labourer and the exploited tenant. The fox too, intellectuals insisted, was an exploited beast, reared so that it could be hunted, killed when it could run no more and the pack closed in to tear it to pieces. That the fox-hunter was himself being hunted never seems to have entered the heads of the anti-bloodsport campaigners. Sublimated hunting is harmless. Financiers and fore-runners in the rat race do it every day and no one sees blood! Now, in the latter part of the twentieth century the RSPCA condemns the foxhunt and, it must be assumed, bloodsport of any kind. That a concern for what happens in the hunting field is paradoxical when there are more serious crimes against animals moved by road and rail, in battery houses and abattoirs escapes notice of many old ladies who contribute to the funds of the society. It is not wrong to make use of animals, only to hunt them! It is not wrong to mutilate a cow or allow a laying hen to become deformed in a battery cage. It is wrong to chase a fox whether it is killed or not. It is wrong to enjoy hunting, which is the very nub of the whole thing. The odd thing is that both factions involved are minorities.

14

Horsepower Takeover

T HERE WAS nothing precipitate about what happened when '*horsepower*' took over even in the great farmland of America and Canada, but on the plains where the wheat was grown the early tractors took to the territory with little difficulty because it was flat. Neither Canadians nor Americans could ever be said to be slow to appreciate new devices or new methods. If they occasionally looked back it was to the old hard way, and to the suffering built into the life of pioneers who were their ancestors. They had blessed McCormick and the binder. They had suffered the hardships which this machine had inflicted upon them, despite its way of turning standing wheat into neatly tied sheaves. They had harrowed and cultivated in a whirl of dust for too long. There were few machines except the binder and a light cultivator or two that allowed the driver of a team to ride. The tractor came to put an end to so much toil and sweat that a man who didn't buy one would be left behind. There was no question of the American or Canadian farmer being left behind. A team of horses could plough for a week to achieve what a tractor plough accomplished in a single day. The horsepower plough turned the subsoil when needed to do so. It moved on like a lumbering buffalo and it was as powerful. Every prairie farmer recognized the revolution almost from the minute it began. Tomorrow's world would be one of much faster cultivation and faster and more economical harvesting, once the reaping machine was modified and its proper potential achieved. Modifications would hardly stop for a quarter of a century or more.

The small-scale enterprise of the average British farmer and the nature of that economy made those who first considered the tractor think very hard. It was a heavy brute. It might strip their shallow soil from rock. It had large drive wheels likely to plough furrows even when it wasn't hauling the plough. It took a lot of room in which to turn round. Its exact wheel base had been less important when it operated on vast fields. There were some places where its very weight would make it a runaway and others where it might topple on to its side. Moreover, since it was an entirely new animal in the stable, the horse know-how of their men when it came to the staggers, glanders, grease or swollen shoulders suddenly became useless. What was needed was a mechanically-minded operator! The whole tradition of farming in Britain had been so closely tied to the draught animal that it was no idle question to ask where would all the mechanically-minded drivers come from. What would happen to the discard, the redundant men? There was another much more significant aspect of the whole thing and that was that the man who bought one of the new monsters could use very few of his old implements on the drawbar of the tractor. Lever-controlled, walk-behind machinery would be useless. Even the old horse binder, adapted to be hauled by a tractor, would need two men to operate it instead of one. It still needed a man on the high seat to work the various levers and handles controlling the depth of cut or putting the machine in or out of gear. The old farmers looked back. The modern farmer looked forward. Neither saw exactly what had to happen. The machine had taken charge of man. He was caught up in the thing from the start.

Perhaps the people with less anxiety than anyone connected with agriculture were the makers of machinery. They had problems to solve, of course. What would have to come was a machine for the land, a light tractor that could turn round even more neatly than a plodding team of Shires. It would have to crawl up hills or rattle along pulling a veritable train of harrows and discs. They had to sell the new tractor but then they would sell all that went with it! The old farmers had never done anything in a hurry. They spent little money on new machinery. What they had inherited were generally very robust implements which the blacksmith was able to maintain when they needed attention. There was no such thing as spares back-up. There had never been any need for it. The olden day implement business wasn't something remote but almost a local industry. The simple kind of machinery the horse-age needed could be bought at a local depot. It was iron-shod. Only under the very roughest use did it break, and then the smith could weld it or effect a stout repair. He put shoes on their horses. He could do most things to keep a binder rolling. The tractor ploughed faster and turned at least two furrows at a time but was the ploughing as good? Would the new way prove as much of a nine-day wonder as the steam plough? The old men believed what they wanted to believe, and the young ones did exactly the same, forgetting or ignoring the fact that here was a great capital investment the like of which farming had never had to contemplate before. Every implement, to do proper justice to the system, would have to be one specially designed for the tractor! The banker would decide the rate of progress.

Britain had emerged from the First World War with so many mechanical lessons to be learned and digested that revolution on the land was slower than in America. Farming in Britain was at far too low an ebb for anyone to think about investing in a completely mechanical set-up. The wonderful thing about the workhorse was that it could be bred without capital. The time from its being foaled until it was in chains or shafts could be as little as two years. It would plod on for nearly twenty. In that time more horses could be bred. All horses needed was grass, oats and stable room. Rather heavy tractors with American names appeared here and there at first. Getting one was a regular market-place topic of conversation that went with much sighing, sucking on pipes and shaking of heads. A man who thought of getting a tractor also dreamed of getting 'the electricity in', buying a motor car, having the telephone. How would he do it with milk prices so impossibly low and arable farming in the doldrums? Only the dreamer himself could explain because only he could dream his way through the hard facts of life.

Designers of farm machinery were not so dull as to think that what served the purpose in America would be good enough for land in Britain. Although there were different problems in different parts of the country what was needed was general purpose equipment and light tractors. Time is in the end what farming is really about. A man succeeds or fails as a result of the pace he manages to maintain. To get the hay off a field while the sun shines, to cut and cart the grain in the minimum number of days, to get all the ploughing done in the shortest possible time. These are things not simply economic but highly satisfying. When they are accomplished the great risk is reduced. The farmer has always lived under the threat of natural disasters—rainstorm or drought, famine and sometimes, of course the old biblical law that says there is a time to sow and a time to reap. When time runs out there is natural disaster. Wheat cannot be harvested in winter. It is too late to plant barley in midsummer. The whole agony of the horse age and the days of the ox had been in this simple truth. Tractor salesmen pointed to sturdy controls, the cost of fuel, the tremendous takeoff power of the machine, and ways it could be put to use to drive a score of things a farmer had never been able to operate with horses. The idea was already sold in America and Canada where the binder was no more. A new kind of harvester was on the way, the combine, but what did the combine do? It made the steam threshing outfit look as old-fashioned as the penny-farthing bicycle because the direction of feed had been changed: the corn that toppled behind the knives went right on to be fed into the threshing machine. There were no sheaves to be set up in stooks. The rich, hard wheat grain spewed into an accompanying wagon or gushed into a hopper and filled sacks. A long worm of battered wheat straw lay on a longer stubble than the McCormick had left but the field was almost as tidy as the old-fashioned farmer's rickyard in October when all the thatching was done. The straw might have to be elevated and baled, or set on fire to put potash back into the ground, but the threshing was done right there on the prairie. No one worked in a whirlwind of chaff. No one forked sheaves until the sweat ran into his eyes. The harvest bug didn't bite. There were no rats to be killed when a rickbutt was forked over. A practical farmer could appreciate what all this meant and would be sure to see that he couldn't afford not to have the things that would make life bearable.

There were a great many implements of different sorts that were the concern of men whose livelihood depended on particular crops. What use was it to speed up cultivation without speeding up planting? The great cabbage field could be ploughed with the same plough that ploughed the wheatfield, but how to speed up planting and cultivation of the vast market garden? The tractor had to straddle rows. Planters had to be carried with the machine. Peas could be sown but they had to be cut and threshed. The tank and the half-tracked army vehicle inspired the designer to produce a crawler tractor. The sheer waste of time and effort involved in the old up-and-down way of ploughing rigs with draining furrows, all to the pole measurement, made the designer work on the reversible plough. When the Second World War was being fought the problem was no longer how to make a good tractor or a tractor-driver out of an oldtime horseman or ploughman, but how to replace him with a landgirl. In France Hitler underlined the fact that traction was everything. This was the horsepower age. The pace of the horse was far too slow for the Blitzkrieg, although even the Wehrmacht still had horse-drawn equipment.

Offered the combine as a replacement for his old binder however, even the wealthy farmer would hesitate at the price he would have to pay. Such a mammoth of a machine must stand idle for most of the year, though it makes short work of a field of corn and the business of threshing. Not every field a man has will carry such a weighty piece of machinery however. A combine may bog down. It might also have to make a somewhat extravagant entry into a field or destroy part of the crop when called upon to negotiate obstacles. The combine cut a wider swath than the old-fashioned binder but the old binder could be set on transport wheels and brought side-on through gates. The big combine couldn't be contracted or taken apart. Gateways had to be widened to accommodate even the small model. The large combine cried out for larger fields. Trees in the field had to be felled and their stumps grubbed out. Hedges likewise had to be uprooted to make two strips into one, letting the monster run farther without having to turn around. In the process, of course, there was the great drawback in the destruction of windbreaks. Barley had never been a very strong-in-the-straw crop. It would go down in a wind even when it was being cut, although the combine was more concerned with the gathering of grain than making straw bales!

It was no wonder that while the modern, forward-looking farmer was hurrying to do everything the machine wanted, he began to reap a kind of harvest he hadn't expected—soil erosion and the loss of fertilizer even as he had it deposited on the field, for the wind carried it away and built it again in miniature drifts. The old farmer, the diehard, sighed for the good old days but he 'got the electricity in' and the telephone. He equipped himself for the deepfreeze kitchen. He banished the gramophone. He would stop telling the tale in the end and have someone else's fantasy put before him by television. His stable emptied, he rummaged for old harness brass and hames to hang on the wall or sell to the dealer in curios. He bought his motor car. It was generally a solid, unpretentious Austin or Morris rather than a Ford. He began to take a calf to market in it, popping the beast in a sack tied at its neck with baler twine. He had been forced to accept the horsepower takeover. He was able to get into town and back home again in less than an hour. Once he would have lost half a day, but now his whole enterprise depended on paraffin, diesel oil and petrol. Rated horsepower responded to the pressure of his foot on brake or accelerator but it was no use crying 'whoa!' for the beast had no ears.

Without doubt the most radical change brought to the field by the tractor was the harvester. The tractor plough had been demonstrated in America early in the twentieth century, around 1910, when three tractors together hauled a gang of fifty ploughs to turn an acre of land in four and a half minutes; but the combined harvester-thresher had been used more than thirty years before this—in the wheatfields of the Pacific coast of America. The combine became a practical proposition at least for the agricultural engineer to work on in the last decade of the nineteenth century. In course of time the original steam traction outfit gave place to the internal combustion engined tractor. What was first of all a very heavy thing was scaled down. The iron wheels of the early models were finally changed for solid rubber and then pneumatic tyres. Almost every item that went with the light engine was designed to suit it. Agricultural engineering had already been accepted as a distinct branch of engineering technology. Men with considerable education and mechanical knowledge now looked at everything the farmer did or needed doing. This meant a close study of the way things had been done in the past and the need to do them in that particular way when the horse had given way to horsepower. Subsoil could be ploughed much easier than before. Ploughing and harvesting were going to be quicker, but the use of tine harrows, disc harrows, seeders, drills, scarifiers, swath turners, tedders, rollers and other

implements had to be studied. Many of them now had to be styled
to suit a method of operating in which the driver of the machine
looked behind for more than half the time. The very thought of a
ploughman looking back to see what he had done would have made
the Victorian farmer flinch! The even furrow turned two at a time
might please the man eager to get his winter wheat drilled, but it
wasn't ploughing to the last of the horse ploughmen still competing
in ploughing matches—but not in their own parishes or even in their
own counties.

What lay behind this relentless change was a matter of pure eco-
nomics. People who had been leaving the land for decades prior
to the advent of the tractor and the combine had gone to live in
towns and urban communities. They still needed to be fed. The
new machines made more people redundant in the country and
enslaved them in the town. They had become producers of everything but their daily bread. Only the tractor rolling off the production line could work fast enough and economically enough to feed
them all. There was a growing need for greater productivity from
the land, alongside a diminished need for casual labour. The services
of migrant workers weren't called for except perhaps in the great
fruit orchards, hopfields and the large market gardens where no one
seemed to be able to solve the problem of picking brussels sprouts.
Farmworkers began to be thinned out. Old horsemen faded away,
saddened at the thought that the stable had been converted into
an implement shed housing a foul-smelling tractor. Young farmworkers scrambled upon the seats of tractors, operated elevators and
balers as though they had been born to it and worked a shorter day.
The field was a lonely place in which to work without a living
creature to keep the tractor driver company but the loneliest job
in the world was on the combine. It was a massive piece of
machinery that rumbled and rattled along, a grotesque blind insect
of gigantic proportions. Sometimes harvest went on by-lamplight.
The headlights of a combining contractor's machine swept the field
and illuminated the ash tree and made the owl blink. There was
no hazard in the night-time dew. There were no canvas sheets to
shrink as there had been on the binder but a man could travel up
and down for days on end without exchanging a word with anyone.
The happy harvest helpers were long gone. There was no tea in

the hedgeside, no corn dolly in the last cut and, after the plague, not even a rabbit to run before the knives. It must be said that the man who remained to work with the new implements proved himself to be something of a mechanic and one willing to learn. He took his seat with more confidence than many a youthful horseman. He made the tractor dance along the rough road. He swept it backwards into its shed and ran it out through bales of hay or oil drums. Only once in a while did he hitch it to a low load and find that it reared up, not quite like a horse on hindlegs, but like a child's toy. When it fell on its back it generally killed its driver. Accidents of this sort made the designers work on the thing to save a driver from his own folly and prevent him from being crushed when the tractor toppled sideways. A very much over-powered machine set to haul a very heavy object uphill would tend to revolve round the drive and fall back like a beetle climbing a mound.

Old Hodge, made redundant in his generation, had no opportunity to rush along lanes on tractors or test them against his beloved horses. His cottage was generally a tied one and when he could no longer do a day's chores of one sort or another he had to go.

It wasn't just Hodge and the plough team he had worked for almost all of his life that had to go. It was the horse, everywhere except on the race course, the hunting field and the riding stable. There were still a great many horses doing a day's work for industry of one sort or another. Every one of them, like the milk on the doorstep, came from the country. Every one of them had been bred for his task. The coal lorry was still pulled by a horse in the nineteen-thirties and milk and bread were carried to the suburbs of every sizeable town by horse-drawn vans. The brewers were proud of their horse teams. The horse pulled the laundry van and the greengrocer's cart while electric tramcars sped past and the last of the steam-traction engines hauled vast wagonloads of flour from northern mills to London and other big cities. There were still horses pulling barges along the canals. People were used to the sound of the horse on the roads when it was already a rather lonely animal on a farm that had gone in for one of the first tractors. The faithful old horse plodded on through the Second World War but always in smaller numbers. The speed at which commerce had to move, like the speed at which harvest had to be got in, was something neither the Shire nor the sturdy cob could achieve. For a short time a ghost horse clopped on the streets of suburbia at dawn. The multiple dairies still using hundreds of horses, put rubber tyres on the milk float and there was an uncanny sound of hoofbeats without wheels that suggested Turpin was rising again, or some headless horseman was on his way to a haunting. The cities had stables of great size. Even the railways stuck to the horse for delivering goods from the station until the lessons of two wars could no longer be ignored and horse and horseman had to be put out to grass. A little later they would get rid of the pony down the pit in most coalfields. The canal boat would be taken in tow and make a grand prow wave as it sped on to Birmingham and the towpath would be left to the fisherman. Thereafter the carter, urinating against his wheel, might no longer relieve himself with impunity. If he did so he might have the policeman scratching his head over the offence of indecency. The policeman too, would never again appear in the Chief Constable's office to be commended for stopping a runaway, a thing the old-time policeman often did in the days of the horse-bus and the old horse-tram. In the country the old women would look in vain for those big horsemushrooms that fried so well with a rasher of bacon.

It was a lively world, the new world of rapid progress everywhere. It was contracting every day it might have seemed to anyone who paused to look around. The horse had been passed by everything on wheels and the wheelwright was almost out of business. The blacksmith scrapped his old hearth with the manually-operated bellows and, getting the electricity in, installed a blower but he didn't do much with implements as the years went by. He no longer had a midden at his door. He had a trolley with an acetylene outfit on it, gas cylinders from the British Oxygen Co. and people brought him little jobs to do on their old cars when they broke down, jobs the garage mechanic really couldn't tackle because they were structural. The horse, when he came to the end of his time was put out to pasture by the sentimentalists but generally tottered off to the knacker who quickly converted the old beast into hide and bones and meat to be processed for dog food and called animal product. The motor car didn't live as long as a horse. It cost a great deal more. It was an expendable piece of transport. It rusted like an old salmon tin. Its body couldn't be processed or even buried very effectively. The tractor would wear out too. Where it rested no mushrooms grew but the ground was permanently polluted by a sludge deposit. Since its lifespan was a little longer—it trundled into old age displaying the infirmities of the old farm labourer—it passed from hand to hand until at last it rested in some outhouse corner of the farm steading, its old-age odour of diesel becoming stronger and dust covering its battered skeleton.

The transformation the new harvester had wrought in the green and pleasant land was noticed by naturalists. The straw-burning that followed in its wake, the destruction of the long stubble by fire not only took away the cover that had formerly sheltered game and small birds. It scorched the earth in the process of giving it potash and killed a great many useful insects and larvae. The threshed wheat or barley had to be kept free of weeds and spraying completed the treatment. No one thought that these weeds were an important part of the nitrogen cycle, the natural manufacture of essential nitrogen by particular plants. They were not encouraged to look into this, for manufacturing nitrogen was a great department of the chemical industry! There was no need any more for the haphazard processes of nature, either the manuring of fields from the midden or the by-blows of wind-carried weed.

The motor car went faster and faster. The tractor plough and the combine rumbled on. Everyone who could afford a car bought one. A few sentimentalists looked at the now rare animal, the working horse with no work to do. No one cared to say that we were committed to the internal combustion engine, permanently settled in the driver's seat. There was no other way ahead and no question of stopping this particular runaway. The sobering truth was that we were also committed to oil in one form or another, and we had none. Our transport would come to a complete standstill and our electricity supply could be reduced to next to nothing spread over the whole country if oil supplies were cut off. We couldn't raise a crop without tilling the field in the old peasant way of cultivation. We couldn't produce horses overnight though we could turn out hundreds of motor cars in a week. The horse had been able to carry so much and had cost so little to run. Slow though the old way had been, it had had a sound economic basis. We had fed the horse corn and grass. It had done its day's work and provided manure for the field. The motor car was beginning to pollute the air and congest the roads and everyone insisted upon having his own carriage. Everyone was a squire! Everyone had the right to the same freedom of movement along the road. Now and again, encountering the horse from a riding school or ridden by a member of the hunt, the blood of the motorist would run to his head at the very thought of the intrusion of a horse on the highway. The fast sports car came screeching into the carpark of the old coaching inn, the Horse Shoes, the Nag's Head, the Black Horse or the Four-in-Hand, and no one paused to think what the names meant any more than the man who lived in a mews thought of the word's association with falconry! The horse was too slow for this world, even too slow for a funeral. The undertaker resented having to feed the black horse between committals. The man who could manage a pair had climbed down from the box to find a job somewhere else. The harness was turning green. The collar backing was moth-eaten or mice-nibbled and the stuffing coming out. The carriage hearse was obsolete without the horses. No one was concerned to breed a black horse any more and only men who were faithful to draught horses continued to breed them for show, like ornamental fowl and other 'quaint' survivals of the glorious past.

No one seems to have noticed that farming has sub-contracted its main enterprise in so many ways that the business bears little relation to what it was when the yeoman sat at the head of his table with half a dozen hired men, each with a different part to play, eating their dinner. Ploughing is often sub-contracted in the horsepower age. Harvesting and threshing have been combined and an outsize replica of the threshing machine, which the steam engine used to haul round the country, has been modified to do everything at once. The combine sub-contractor is in business booking for harvesting all round the county as the threshing contractor once booked customers for threshing. The contractor's men are the same kind of countrymen as ever, but mechanically minded. They once changed teams at noon to have fresh horses for the long hard afternoon in the field. Now they rest the combine for five or six hours when it overheats, as it sometimes does. When they have ploughed, they cultivate and roll, harvest and bale, spread muck, plough out the ditches, cut the hedges, pump away the pig slurry, build barns of bales and set to ploughing again not perhaps on the same farm, but somewhere in the same parish. Half a dozen hired men and half a dozen hired machines are at work. The contractor has a great yard full of plant for every task. This is not to say that the farmer is left with nothing to do. He somehow has his hands as full as ever but he has ten acres he cannot get round to be ploughed by a sub-contractor, or his midden moved so that he can make alterations in his yard. He must have the shearing squad to shear his sheep. He calls the contractor to come and run his stock to the sale. The country road is busy with tankers and lorries, cattle transports and big lumps of machinery crawling from one place to another. Even the old horse, broken to shafts, steady in the face of the motor car, would show the whites of his eyes and set his ears flat on his head to see the reptilian excavator lifting its ugly head from the ditch, its jaws dripping water and masking in green weed as it munches on mud and gravel the old ditcher once cleared. The smell of the countryside is different. New-mown hay is gone in a few days. The meadow-sweet doesn't grow in the ditch. The crab apple and the blackthorn have been grubbed out. The fume of the motor car poisons the blackberry and the wild strawberry—if the roadside hedgemower happens to miss shaving them away!

15

The New Ways

W HAT MODERN agriculture consists of is a sort of hydra-headed industry ranging from the care of animals to large-scale market gardening. The term farming now applies to many minor enterprises beyond the everyday use of the word. What happened after the horsepower day dawned affected every branch of agriculture. The advance, a war communiqué would have said, was on all fronts. There were milestones. In dairy farming, for instance, there was the change to tested milk. This didn't happen all over the country in the same year, or even within a decade, but the change was inevitable for those who wanted to get the best from their investment. It was not because of any edict that the old ways had to be abandoned. Those who persisted in the old way through lack of vision or even for sentimental reasons would pay, and few farmers could afford to be sentimentalists. A lot of the old ways were no more humane than the new ones. The old farmer had bled his pig to death and cut the throat of a duck to make sure its flesh was as white as possible. He shot his horse if it broke a leg, because a horse with a broken leg has nowhere to go, but many a time he rushed to get the butcher with a humane killer to put down a sick cow. This wasn't out of compassion but in order to make something out of the beast by forestalling death. The economic facts of survival made him this kind of man. He wasn't playing at being a farmer. He was compelled to do what he did. He was inevitably compelled to look for the easier way. Haysel and corn harvest were not the ad-man's dream of sunshine, fluttering butterflies and acres of waving wheat dotted with poppies. They were labour and sweat. The machine had banished the pain and suffering. The scientist told Giles that there were other, easier, more sensible ways. Being unscientific had been at the root of his trouble and the cause of his frustration. The economist said it had been low prices and lack of capital. He was now seeing the benefit of the culling of his milking herd and the double-fencing of his fields. He had some hope of living happily ever after on his milk cheque! If he could persuade the bank to stand by him there were all sorts of things he might do to improve his lot. He must put away peasant outlook and submit himself to close scrutiny.

When they put a magnifying glass on what Giles was doing, and a microscope on his crop and his stock, it was plain that hardly anything was as good as it might have been. He needed more than ever to protect crops from pests and viruses, to have his soil analysed, his sheep injected against the things that plagued them, his calves, pigs and chickens all treated with different serums or antibiotics. Most ways of doing things were being intensively researched in colleges and institutions and the chemical industry was busy researching on its own account. The new way was in every direction! The scientist told him what wheat to grow, the best strain of barley to stand the wind, how many hours of light in a production-line hen battery a laying pullet would need to achieve the norm. There were ways of handling poultry the old farmer's wife could never have dreamed of—keeping them on deep litter or, better still, in a battery cage. Losses at lambing time could be reduced by more intensive care. Sheep scab could be eradicated. Fowl pest and swine fever called for new techniques in managing and feeding birds and pigs. What wasn't out of date was going to be very soon. To stay in the game Giles would turn his piggery into something much cosier than the house his old father had lived in. The pigs would have electric light, a carefully measured ration of food, be weighed as often as a woman in pregnancy, and produce exactly the kind of bacon or ham the market called for. The feeding chart would tell Giles the quantity of balanced food and another would convert these figures into dead weight or some other vital factor. Giles would put the old farm book away. It had always been about as businesslike as the old draper's bundle of bills. What was needed was order and system. Giles would need an accountant to tell him whether he was profitably fattening a pig or not. The accountant wouldn't need to see the pig, or know one end of it from the other so long as he could draw up profit and loss accounts.

The process of persuading the farmer to go over to one way or another was essentially gradual in the beginning. He was being brain-washed and educated. He was also being intimidated and tempted in turn. He looked about and saw what he must do to stay in business. He talked to the bank and listened to the salesmen. They told him that theirs were no wild dreams. They could prove everything with statistics. They had pictures of the thing done on model farms. One day, they said, smiling, he would actually sit in his centrally heated farmhouse watching a radio-controlled cultivator crawling up a field and make it turn on the headland by pushing a button. It made yesterday seem like the Stone Age. Imagine a man working out there with a horse and a set of harrows or forking loose hay to another man building a rick! It all belonged in the world of straw-chewing Hodge in his smock, hiring himself according to how much beer or cider the master would provide! The horsepower age had put paid to all that and made it as quaint and unrealistic as the stocks and the treadmill. The conversion of man and master took place without the slightest hesitation. Hodge wanted to be involved in things where for generations he had simply been a pair of hands and a strong back to hold a plough or load swedes in a cart. His employer—the word master had gone out of date now—wanted a better way of life for himself and his family. He was entitled to it. He was after all, a prime producer, as important to the economy as the man operating a machine at the coalface or making bread. He was being listened to by the politicians. All he needed was a guarantee, a fair revision of prices from time to time. He reminded them that he invested in farming. Everything he had was in plant, in crops or in stock. He didn't always own the land and here and there he farmed land that was uneconomic. The experts told him how many acres he needed to make a living. The Ministry told him what his average income was and how many men and machines he used. He sent his son to agricultural college and the young man came home and told him there were still better ways.

To begin with, the average farmer needed to look ahead a great deal more than his father had ever done. The new ways almost invariably called for new and expensive plant. It wasn't possible to switch from one thing to another without suffering considerable loss. A farmyard could soon become cluttered with redundant equipment no one else in the district wanted to buy and the tallest nettles would never hide. The fact was that the farmyard had been modernized until it looked more like a factory. It was concreted wall to wall—the picturebook modern farm of course—and had its machinery in ordered rows. It had its fuel tank to keep the tractors running, its piped water, its silo and its great iron barns. There wasn't a wheel from a haywain to be seen anywhere, nor a horseshoe nailed to a door. The old rickyard had been eliminated from the face of the earth by a grader.

Even although old Giles had been an essentially practical, unsentimental man he had drawn the line at certain things. A sense of fitness had made him reluctant to dock the tails of his plough teams. His image of an Ayrshire or Jersey cow was a beast with horns on its head, but they told young Giles that stock could be better managed without horns. The day when men talked of a cow to so many acres might have meant something in survival terms but it was possible to keep a great many more cows on a farm than in the days of hand-milking and the old conventional shippon. Keeping animals in closer proximity and feeding them standing-in, a cow was better without horns. Like most females, the cow sometimes finds too many of her own sex more than she can bear and uses her horns aggressively. Dehorning might not result in peace and harmony but it avoided bloodshed. Taking the horns off a cow was less of a mutilation than castrating a calf or a lamb. They took the beaks off pheasants, didn't they? The sultan of the East did something of the sort to his harem attendants and the means justified the end. Scientists were doing amazing things with animals. A cow with a lid in her back allowed them to sample the stomach residue and work out the real value of her input over so many hours! The cow lived indoors for the rest of her life and it was all in the interest of progress and profit. Farming depended on what came after the decimal point. It was a science, and at last the scientists were having their day. If they were denied the world would starve.

Only to the sentimentalist is the sound of the cockcrow a modern loss. The nostalgic picture he carries in his head is one of brown and white hens picking their way about a green field. The cock crows in the morning and at intervals through the day. It all goes with the singing of the scythe shearing stalks, of course, and the endless sound of the grasshopper. In a world of screaming jets and snoring juggernauts streaming along broad highways the sentimental picture is absurd. The free-range bird is not an economic prospect. It is something for the faddist, the experts would say. It may lay an egg with a brighter yellow yolk but the chemist can take care of that. If the consumer wants a brown egg the genetics expert tells the producer how to breed a bird that will lay nothing but brown eggs. Who needs a cockerel, let alone the sound of its monotonous crowing? Even a schoolboy knows that a hen doesn't need to be mated in order to lay an egg. The cockerel only needs to be cultivated for breeding the chick to be reared for the battery. All the fancy breeds of fowl our fathers kept were a self-indulgence. Most of them were inefficient layers and not very good table birds. The whole business of poultry-keeping had been haphazard and wasteful. No hen should ever be kept into its old age. It becomes tough. It ceases to lay. It has to be buried. The modern strain of bird will lay more eggs in its one year of life than the free range hens kept by nineteenth-century Giles or Hodge laid in their whole lifetime! The new strain of bird will lay an egg almost every day of the year and turn on a spit or become a broiler immediately its peak has passed. Waste not and want not had been the motto of the Victorians. The old way was in contradiction and at last the answer has arrived. A bird kept in light, warm and well-fed, doesn't use its energy in looking for food and scratching around middens. It couldn't lay away in a deep litter shed or, better still, a battery. Here is the ultimate in egg-production and hen-management, for the bird is fed exactly the right amount of food. The food contains everything it needs to keep it healthy. It has fresh water. It is warm and already treated for pests and parasites. It proves itself by laying as though operated by a time switch. Moreover, in answer to those sentimentalists who saw something like the galleries of Sing Sing or Alcatraz in the cage system, it is a happy bird. Only a happy bird lays.

There is a small distortion of the truth in this but only a pedant would argue that a disturbed or frightened bird will go off the lay and can withhold the egg at will. The battery hen, like any prisoner, quickly becomes accustomed to the cage. She lays and goes on laying because light, temperature and diet have all been contrived to encourage the natural function. In the process, however, two or three other things happen naturally. The bird's beak tends to grow like a neglected toenail. Its claws grow round the mesh of the cage upon which it crouches. Its legs lose their ability to support the body, and the feathers on its head, neck and belly are worn away by its attempts to move and feed itself through the bars of its prison. These horrors overlooked, it cannot be denied that there is a wonderful economy in having a bird that produces the maximum number of eggs in return for the expensive food it has to have to do so, and then immediately becomes an important item of food. What would an egg cost without these highly intensive methods? Who would pay for it? There would surely be shortage and high prices. Perhaps it is a case of the end justifying the means once again but even with the method prices are maintained in a time of glut. The egg is stored. The battery bird does its stint and everyone can have chicken in the basket.

It is unfair to suggest that this kind of thing is the work of young Giles. Like the rest of his generation, he is caught up in something evolving from all that had gone before, and morals, as Shaw said through one of his characters, are for those who can afford them. Factory farming is a dirty word. The system has been examined by quite brilliant scientists given to looking at cause and effect without making emotional conclusions. It isn't what a nation with a conscience would like but man manipulates the different forms of life that fall within his power and we all live on some other form of life. Cruelty needs to be defined and when it is, it can be seen everywhere. It troubles some people to see a bloody steak but they are less troubled if it is well done and this is not entirely a matter of taste. The outlook of the townsman is tempered by the fact that he sees what is going on in the country and the farm but he doesn't associate himself with killing or the exploitation of animals and birds. His milk comes out of a bottle. His steak out of the freeze room. His egg out of an eggbox bought in the supermarket. The whole farming enterprise it seems could be operated on the lines of those idyllic television commercials and Giles could go back to being a wholesome, honest country bumpkin.

Whatever was the right way, this second phase of the revolution in farming methods was accompanied by the death of the steam engine. The steam plough had gasped its last on the headland long since. It had been jostled out of the way when it hauled the threshing machine. It was redundant on the road whether as a traction engine hauling flour or gas clinker, or as a steam roller. It was finally to be taken off the railway where it had rocked and rumbled along for a century and a quarter hauling coal from Newcastle to make steel in the Midlands, carrying cattle to city slaughterhouses, and men to war. As it had overtaken the horse, the internal combustion engine began to come on after the steam locomotive, driving it to the extremities of the unprofitable branch lines and promising one day to make the journey from Edinburgh to London faster than the famous Flying Scotsman. The passion for things powered by oil or electricity was as ungovernable in twentieth-century man as the fancy for steam had been in the Victorian age. It developed blindly, transporting goods that were already being carried by the railways, outflanking the steam engine in a curious way and making coal no longer necessary. The farmer didn't need to cart coals from the country station any more. He bought his wife an electric stove or one that was oil-fired. He received his supplies on his doorstep, seed, basic slag, pigwire, timber, all delivered by road. The system was entirely to his liking. He lost no more time in carrying things. The branch line of the railway, at one time a vital artery, began to show rust. The depot became deserted. New centres of distribution were being set up by the fertilizer companies, the seedsmen, the suppliers of farm equipment and ironmongery. All of them operated with road transport. The telephone made everything simple. Great articulated lorries roared along new motorways with everything the farmer could desire or the depot could stock. The railway was nobody's concern. The shareholders were faceless, and not likely to riot if no dividends were paid for the whole system had been losing money even in the day of the horse. All at once it was discovered that a steam locomotive needed coaling depots and had to get up steam before it could move. It needed watering places along the way. Its smoke fouled the new railway stations. Oil was much better and electricity, depending on oil, was better still. The countryside didn't need its branch lines. So few people lived out there that it was uneconomic to run a service for them but the branch lines might be used for roads. The steel could be salvaged. The little old station with the slat fence could make a wonderful cottage, as fascinating as a converted windmill or oasthouse turned into a middle-class, weekend dwelling. Once again the die was cast. This was an age when everyone wanted to be able to ride behind his own grey mare. Everyone must have his own brougham and the internal combustion engine had made this possible. That there was only so much room didn't bother the man who bought the motor car. He could thread his way out into the country. What was needed was a better road system, even if it cut slices off good arable land, even if the fume of the engine polluted the air, even if it was hard to say exactly where a lot of people were bound when they took to the road. The farmer wasn't going to be left behind but he objected to the encroachment of the town and housing estates being built on his precious acres, for every day the experts were telling him just what his income would be from one form of agriculture or another on a given acreage.

Mrs Giles had more than her oil-fired cooker. She had the blessing of the deep freeze and she had a ready means of transport. She might make a hobby now of some of the things her mother and grandmother had done of necessity, but she was unlikely to bother to salt a ham, make jam in great quantities, or put up goose grease against a cold on the chest any more than she would make her own soap. Even baking would be more of a self-indulgence, a creative outlet, than a routine, daily task to feed a large number of labourers. She wouldn't buy a chest of tea, a sack of sugar, flour or oatmeal. She would run the brake to the supermarket on the edge of town and come back loaded with everything she needed, including bacon and ham and cheese, all of which had once been local products. There was no virtue in being old-fashioned. It was eccentric to insist on the old way. Loath as she might be to part with the brass and copper her mother had treasured she was ready to change the old dresser for a set of kitchen units—if the beef prices continued to hold or potatoes didn't become a glut—and get a new, automatic washing machine. Who was to say a farmer's wife should have less? Who took more risks or worked harder than her husband?

Hodge's wife wasn't quite so comfortably off, of course. There always would be a differential between a man who invested his

labour and one who invested everything he had. The wages of farm
workers would always lag behind those who worked in the car factories but there was nothing to stop the farm worker leaving the
countryside and finding work in the town. All around this had been
happening at an increasing pace for at least a century. It was a question of whether a man chose one way of life or decided to try another.
When the farm worker was able to exert himself and obtain improvement in wages and conditions he too, could have a car of sorts.
His wife found herself looking for a second job, not only because
their joint need, their standard, was higher, but because the same
kind of faceless, far-off authority that had shut the railway and was
contracting the bus service had decreed that the country school was
another inefficient, obsolete institution. The school bus collected
children in the same way that the cattle float picked up sheep for
market and whisked them off to the town. Mrs Hodge could find
herself a job at the filling station along the road or serving at the
modernized inn, where company executives sat long over their fillet
steaks and Beaune and hazily wondered what was going on out there
on the old stubble where the tractor went up and down like a blue-
bottle on the window.

In a very similar way to the Victorian, the twentieth-century Bri-
tisher had become short-sighted on the implication of his way of
life and the standard he exacted from the system. The Victorian
had been unaware how much of his strength, his ability to get by,
depended on the exploitation of India and the empire. What supported the economy was invisible in the mid-nineteenth century but
in spite of the profit from colonial enterprise, times had been far
from easy. In the twentieth century the switch from horse to horsepower, and steam to oil, depended upon the availability of oil and
a low price paid to those countries from which it was extracted. The
great empire had tended to extract useful materials from the
colonies, raw materials which could be processed and sold again,
even basic foods. The native population contributed labour for
which they were paid and therefore they benefited. The account
was square, or so the merchants said. When oil became the mainstay
of industry, agricultural as well as manufacturing, this happened
everywhere at roughly the same time and made it inevitable that
the price would rise. When the people from whose countries the

oil was taken put their hand on the pipe to stop the flow they were like the old farmer's wife taking the goose by the neck. It might well flap and complain. It was in real danger of being killed.

In the circumstances prevailing at this stage in the agricultural revolution, an objective observer might say that things have gone ahead too fast. There is always an inevitable slowing down and sometimes the system must revert to ways it has discarded and methods abandoned. The horse could be brought back. We could harvest without the tractor and the combine. The wheelwright and cart builder could be taught his trade by someone still possessing the skill. The harness-maker could be surrounded by apprentices. We could do it because our forefathers did it. The problems could all be surmounted by a brave and resourceful people. There are those who will make a case for reverting to what was done before the Arab discovered that oil was a better weapon than a muzzle-loader or even a missile. Neither Giles nor Hodge is the man his father was, but a different man produced by a different environment. He doesn't think the same way. The sum he had to add is quite different. There is no longer a peasant labour force. The population to be supported by the land is a great deal bigger than it was in the nineteenth century and the machine belongs on the field however it must be powered. The pyramids may have been built without machines and the great wall of China without mechanical assistance, but the farmworker must have the machine. The population can't live on a bowl of rice a day. Hodge as a mechanic isn't redundant but Hodge the peasant is dead and buried. Old Giles bought a youthful scarecrow for tuppence a week. He ate his cheese without paring away the rind in a day when sailors froze on the rigging of ships crossing the ocean to bring tea, but we are entering a new world Giles is told, a world of electronics, push-button, lasers, genetics and plant pathology. The problem to be solved is a new way to do without the oil and to change the energy source again! The working horse has been out of date for forty years. The internal combustion engine may not last as long as the horse. The scientist who once frightened the farmer into changing his methods, is frightening him again by saying that a bullock eating grass to produce protein is a highly wasteful creature. There are other ways and more efficient methods—the manufacture of imitation meat, the

processing of soya flour—laboratory beef! People can be educated
to enjoy a taste and taste can be imitated. Flavour can be manufactured and smell can be reproduced! We may eat grass yet without
it passing through the stomachs of the cow or being ruminated by
the lamb. All we may need is a great hayfield but we may not even
need the hayfield in the end. We could live on seaweed. We could
perhaps recycle everything and ourselves become ruminants of a
sort! The chemist claims he has the answer now we have come from
the age of simple mechanics to science. Between the physicist and
the biologist even Giles may be redundant in the end. The oracle
has spoken.

Hodge and Giles, no longer self-sufficient or masters of their own
small domain, have undergone yet another change. They once provided their own entertainment. They sang and danced and they told
tales. One of them played the fiddle or the piano. They went to
whist drives and they played dominoes in the pub. Now they sit
and watch television. The images they might have created in their
minds are put there for them, convincing them that what was old
is inefficient and wasteful. What is new, even if only a theory, is
the thing. What is wrong with life in the country is its slowness,
its lack of activity, its dullness as a man sits on a machine and crawls
from one end of a field to the other and back again. The doctrine
saps the countryman's resistance to change. He is afraid of being
left behind and not taking the new way. He is conscious of the fact
that the townsman has everything his heart could wish for, on tap
and close to his hand. He sometimes thinks he ought to go and
become one of them! 'All mod cons' means everything. He would
only be one more to add to the generations who have migrated, lock,
stock and barrel, to the barbican. What is life in the country when
it comes down to it? It is a day's work out there on the plough.
It is a long journey on the combine. It is eight to ten hours looking
after a herd of prize Friesians. It is a walk over a rough hill looking
for sheep or a day muck-spreading over the stubbles. Once in a while
it is something else, a day's rough shooting with a couple of spaniels
or following the hunt, an agricultural show and free lunch from the
seed firm or the chemical company, the market and a few pints of
bitter in some low-ceilinged old pub.

The new way makes him think the milk cheque isn't reliable and barley beef isn't the answer. He faces price controls and import quotas and Common Market agreements such as his father could never have dreamed of. If he is a small man he hopes he may be able to stay in the business. If he is a big man he is afraid that he has put all his eggs in one basket, or that the politicians who every so often tell him that he is the salt of the earth and the real backbone of the nation, will sell him out for some reason they can't explain except that it was in the national interest. There are too many small farms they tell him when he pleads for something better. His isn't an economic unit. He, like a lot of other people, must accept that he is living in the latter part of the twentieth century when, as never before, things must be economically viable. The word viable is significant. Few things were viable in the Hungry Forties and they weren't much better in the 1930's. What was always needed was the new way but the new way would ultimately mean the end of Giles and Hodge altogether and 'farming' becoming a factory process in its entirety.

16

The Foot Hard Down

I F COBBETT or his ghost could ride on into the twentieth century
the first entry he would make in his diary would surely tell that
his itinerary had been ruined when he was forced off the road
by carriages travelling at high speed. If he did as he had often done,
and attempted to travel across country, he would find himself passing under giant pylons and coming to an abrupt halt at the broad
motorway. His calculations wouldn't be about bushels to the acre,
the price of wheat or wool, but about the good land swallowed up,
not just by the town, but the great arterial roads, motorways as significant on the face of the land as a rainbow in the sky, but permanent and more awe inspiring. Perhaps old Cobbett would have
understood the implement yard of the modern farm, the silo and
the milking parlour, but he would have wondered at the great
excavations for gravel and sand and the opencast coal site would
have taken his breath away. He wouldn't have understood pollution.
It wasn't invented in his day. If man had always been at pains to
protect his crop from the ravages of birds and insect pests and even
in Pliny's time considered this essential to good husbandry, he
hadn't yet asked the chemist for the ultimate weapon.

The changing face of the rural landscape troubled Cobbett. He
bemoaned the derelict mansions with their boarded windows. He
saw a great many empty churches and wondered about the tax the
church levied to support livings from which the parson was often
absent—socializing at the holiday resort or the spa. The good man
was sorry for the poor labourer and critical of the new class of landowners from the city. He was committed to the cause of the farmer
but what he so strenuously deplored was something bearing little

comparison with the change taking place a century later. The face of the whole countryside has now been transformed and the change is not only relentless but a quite irreversible and frightening one. Change is an integral part of our survival. The countryman and the townsman both protest, but they also protest against the weather, our climate, the rate of taxation and a hundred other things about which little can be done. We all protest against everything that separates us from infant security and the familiar surroundings of formative years. Even when the conservationist cries out against the cutting down of a tree or the demolition of a landmark this is what it is about. The tree is old and it is beautiful. It cannot be replaced in a lifetime. Perhaps King Charles hid in its branches, but it hardly matters. The buttercross is also old and the arch in the old town wall belongs to our glorious past. If we lose these things we shall lose tangible history. We are making history, of course, whether we are aware of it or not and we can't live in the museum. We sometimes have to accept the fact that we can't have the old market square *and* the roundabout or flyover. The farmer knows he can't have the line of beeches and plough a thousand acres. The artist loves the birch cluster silhouetted by the morning sun on the black fen, but cabbages are food and we can't live on canvas and paint, even if the artist paints a field of brussels sprouts. If we insist upon preserving yesterday we may have to accept a rather severe limitation of our plans for tomorrow. Our children may want. The Oxfam posters warn us.

In the depths of the rural wilderness we have thousands of relics of yesterday—the windmill, with its sails no longer turning, the watermill with its sluice gate locked by rust and its timber slimed with algae. We can come across the tollhouse where drovers paid their dues. Cobbett's empty churches sit in the same holy silence because they were built to stand for ever. Our inheritance is rich, but we have hardly the time to survey it. The foot that controls our speed is hard down and we are confronted by problems that concern our tomorrows. Our environment travels with us like the background of a car chase simulated by television technicians. All at once someone notices that an ancient thorn hedge is being grubbed out. It was there before the first land enclosures. It was part of the dream world in which we see our great-great-grandfather walking, but it is too late to get the man to hold his hand. The hedge is gone, the trees are felled and the roots dragged out. We might get up a petition to save the old tithe barn. It epitomized the rule of the establishment in the Hungry Forties, but in many of these things the tide is not only flowing round our boots but rising over them. When we apply to the bureaucrat he moves slowly. The cause is lost. When the bureaucrat makes up his mind to do something in spite of us he moves fast and there is a *fait accompli*. He knows there is nothing more dismaying to the citizen. Both he and the politician consider this an ace up their sleeves. If we are to have a green belt—not to produce food so much as to preserve property values for those who live beyond it, the cynic would say, then some unfortunate people must live in higher and higher rookeries. If we are to have national parks the hill farmer must get used to the invading rambler. The rambler must get used to the hostility of the hill farmer. An official will lay down the law. There is no such thing as individual right over land. In the end a faceless civil servant will rule, or perhaps the computer will whirl to dispense programmed justice, fining the transgressor, painlessly and secretly debiting his bank account for letting sheep stray, or preventing someone from marching through a field.

The most obvious side effect of the great rush ahead is the change in the rural population and the way in which it makes its living. Although the farmer farms and his employee operates his machinery much of the countryside within fifty miles of the city and a few miles of most of the motorways has become dormitory. The commuter puts a premium on the country cottage, even when he may lack the money to build himself a villa in some well-wooded tract of land. The picturesque cottage, the mill, the oasthouse only need to be surveyed by the architect to reveal potential as a minor development project. The renovator discovers a bonanza. It becomes a creative outlet, a more than profitable indulgence, especially when there are grants to help it all along. The old beams of the cottage are pickled, the range is torn out. The whole place gets a facelift and the Jaguar looks good on the newly-gravelled drive. Town and country planning people approve. The assessment goes up and almost everyone is pleased. What has happened can't be bad in a place where there was formerly a lurching privy in an elderberry clump and a well in which a cat got drowned. All that this kind of thing takes is money, and practically all that was lacking in old Hodge's day was that. The developer, encouraged by the good work he had done, and no one can deny that he has improved everything, applies for another grant to improve another cottage in another place. He sells the first one, repaying the grant to the authority perhaps, and a new weekender moves in. Why shouldn't this happen anyway? The old ruin would soon have crumbled to a rubble of brick and horsehair-bound plaster showing ribs of wormed lath. Instead it has been photographed and sold as a desirable, modernized country cottage, near the motorway, having central heating, oak beams, new thatch and all mod cons. The old villagers look at it with a certain awe. Imagine that old place with double glazing, a wrought iron knocker to be heard all the way up the street, and thick glass whorls to let the light through the door! The crack has gone from the gable and a sports car broods in a prefabricated garage with a throw-up door.

Who are these people? The old countryman must know all about everyone, what they do, how they live and whether they are fools or knaves. The incomers have no trade such as thatcher, cobbler, smith or wheelwright, but then what work would there be for them to do if they had these skills, and what ordinary craftsman could afford such luxuries? They are foreigners, incomers. They never will really belong to the village. They would never have washed their clothes with water from the rain barrel, or filled a kettle from the well after the cat had been fished out of it, though they might have used an Elsan. If they had seen the rats under the old henhouse and one popping out of the thatch they would have left for London that very night. They are stockbrokers, dealers in futures, big executives with three cars and a speedboat to be towed. They tend to become gregarious like rooks, given time, and will take over the pub and the snug on Sunday mornings. They take a pride in their bygones, staddles, cartwheels, a dogcart or even a black-painted gintrap. In some places they raise the cost of living so much that the natives can't afford to stay, but they do bring money and a little colour and excitement to life. They greet young Hodge without seeming to patronize or condescend. He plays a good game of skittles. They always buy him a pint. They know the name of his dog, for knowing names proves that they belong. They have a special 'in' with the locals who can get most things, a sack of potatoes or a side of beef. They meet Hodge and his master and they love the world of the weekend, the simple life perfumed by the scent of burning oak logs. Lambs bleat in the stillness of the night. An owl cries from the ridge of the old barn. What more could a man wish for? Country people know how to live! They keep well clear of the rat race, and this is true. The old countryman knows how to plant a garden, how to manage his few hens, his bees, or the pig he keeps at the bottom of his garden. His livelihood is a bit of this and that, seasonal chores for a farmer friend, a part-time job, casual labour paid for in kind.

The business of survival for those who own neither land nor stock, and will never get rich, calls for a jack-of-all trades kind of ability in a place where craftsmen have faded away. It still takes a skilled thatcher to thatch a cottage but thatches aren't everyday and a good handyman can replace a tile or a slate. The man who can drive a van can find work. All he needs is mobility so long as he can dig a drain, do a bit of passable walling, put a pane of glass in a cottage window or lay a bit of plastic pipe to an outhouse. Such a man needn't fear the taxman overmuch. The farmer knows where to find him when he needs some extra help. If he can strip an electric motor, clean a pump or rig some temporary wiring he is part of the fabric of country life whether he has served his time to a trade or not. He deserves his living and he may pay his way. The weekender more than pays his way. He employs the odd job man's wife to char and look after his property in his absence. He contributes to the wages of the weekend barman. He pays his share of the rates and in an unobtrusive way he works himself into the fabric. In doing so he helps to foster a certain if reluctant tolerance of one world for the other. What the countryman has he would like.

The way of life of the man born in the country is continually being gently adjusted to social and economic change as well as to the renovation of his background, the very topography of his world. What the eye doesn't see, however, the heart doesn't grieve over. There is a great deal that Giles and Hodge don't really see and the weekender never knows about. They have all come into the second half of a century of increasing speed looking for more efficient ways, easier communication, a better and more pleasant living. They have discovered that these things were almost within their grasp with technicians, engineers, chemists and biologists working for them. The weekender materializes on the country scene by virtue of the expressway and the high-powered car and lives out of his deepfreeze by virtue of technology. Hodge has less hardship at calving time or lambing as a result of the research into animal husbandry. His master may calculate his outlay and possible profit margin because someone worked on the design of an electric calculator. Technicians study means and engineers translate them into mechanics. The chemist reminds the farmer that husbandry is not simply breeding animals and growing crops but destroying the things that would become parasites on his labour. The world in which this battle is joined is largely unseen. Its boundaries are undefined and the life cycles of parasites have to be traced so that they can be eliminated. There is nothing new about the principle of plant and animal protection by the use of compounds of one sort or another, any more than there is anything new about the ravages of the leatherjacket, the weevil, the liver fluke, or plant viruses that destroy a crop. The mouse, the rat and the housefly are as easy to see as the sparrow, but hard to kill because they have become conditioned to surviving. They have been trained by force of time and circumstance and they are there because they are survivors. A field of wheat is there because it is cultivated. A field of hay is not just long grass but a selection of special grass or a mixture of grasses that will thrive well on a particular pasture. This is what arable farming is in its essence, but the plague is always in the offing. The battle is not won when the seed germinates or even as the corn rises. The biologist and the chemist have hardly had a hand in the business if they haven't pointed out the weaknesses of particular strains to certain diseases and suggested remedies, preventative medicine, sprays, dustings, inoculations that ensure that when a harmful pest is destroyed, the plant is fit for human consumption. The farmer is a man who plants the field or has a cow inseminated; but behind him, backing him up, saving him from ruin, is the chemist and the researcher.

During the Second World War there came on the scene DDT, a deadly compound that would cure everything, or so it was thought until the common housefly proved itself capable of resisting it, and BHC—benzene hexachloride. These potent and persistent compounds only needed to be accompanied by selective weedkillers to eliminate the risk of failure on the field. Spray a field, dress grain, kill off the unwanted herbage and the job was done! It was a picture that pleased the man in a hurry. It pleased the consumer who imagined that things would get cheaper in the age of insecticides, inoculations, vaccines or serums. Now and again, however, a red light showed. The spray drifted over one crop and fell instead on another.

Light aircraft could swoop as low over a field as a hunting sparrowhawk but they couldn't do anything about the gentle breeze and when the breeze became a gust of wind the spray floated on. Some crops were found to be highly sensitive to sprays that had no harmful effect on other forms of plant life. The chemist looked into all this of course. The man spraying the crop was briefed again or the researcher found a new way of building the protection into the plant through the treatment of its seed. The farmer really didn't know his enemy. He hadn't the very special microscopes to his hand. He would barely have recognized a virus had he looked at one. He didn't need to know about the efficiency of fuel to drive a tractor, any more than he needed to have a knowledge of calculus to put up a barn. But the truth was that very few people knew the ultimate effect of a lot of things being done. There were a number of simple illustrations of chain reaction and indications of a limit to which a new discovery could be relied upon. It was possible to spray a hedgebank and prevent the spread of the seeds of weeds. It was also possible to kill the larvae of insects by using sprays. These things worked and could be seen to be effective by the improvement in the growing wheat or barley. There were no weed seeds in the winnowed chaff but there were drawbacks. Seed-eating birds declined, making the use of the spray more necessary everywhere. The insect pests were eliminated to a lesser degree but the food of insectivorous birds was also eliminated, and those birds were needed on a much wider front. The birds that gleaned poisoned seeds suffered a build-up of toxic substances which killed hawks that preyed on them. The falcon was almost eliminated in his turn. The eggs of peregrines failed to hatch. To some people there seemed a great significance for man himself in such a disaster.

The insect sprays poisoned insects and contaminated bees. The weed sprays destroyed a lot of plants from which bees and other useful pollinating insects derived their food. No one bothered to consider the seriousness of the destruction of pollinating insects and what this might mean to food supplies but there was more to come. The selective weedkillers were selective so far as the man growing a crop was concerned. They were not exactly selective so far as entomology was concerned! The entomologist began to count the butterflies. It didn't require much study to discover that when a plant host to a particular caterpillar is killed off—the nettle supports some of our most beautiful butterflies—that butterfly tended to become a rarity. The bank-nesting wasp and the bumble bee died on the sprayed verges. The wasp is a great predator upon harmful insects. The bumble bee pollinates the clover—that feeds the cow, that gives milk, that feeds the man who sprays the verge. The scientist had no inclination to pursue his study anything like so far! He was the man supplying the ammunition. He didn't want to know how the gun was used, or how many people his bullets might kill. He would have been horrified to find himself accused of killing a red admiral when he was trying to wilt a nettle. He might as well have protested that he had nothing to do with a child dying from drinking paraquat when there was a warning on the container. But it was asking a lot to have *everything* printed on a container—Don't use this liquid to kill your nettles if you like to look at butterflies! Don't use this seed-dressing if you like to see a falcon stooping.—Use it if you want a surplus of grain to feed the starving children of India!

In the early days of miracles they had looked at the grey rat, a pest that infested docks, barns and old buildings of all kinds in which food could be stored. The grey rat spoiled and devoured more food than any other animal pest. It carried disease. It bred up fast. It was a nuisance not only in the barn, but in the hen run. The old types of poison had been useless against it. It could never really be kept in check with poison or trap. It could never be eradicated even by the most lethal of gases, because a few would survive in corners which the gas could not reach. These survivors could breed as fast as the rabbit but the chemist and the pathologist worked on this. The rat had always been in the laboratory for experiment! They decided that it could be killed by dehydration. The rat would take the new bait and simply shrink into the folds of its skin. When it died it looked like an old soft leather purse. They called the miracle Warfarin, and it was a miracle. Deep litter houses that had been tunnelled and almost undermined by rats were cleared of the pests. Rats that had run nose to tail across barn floors became dazed and lethargic and died. The Pied Piper himself couldn't have worked a more astonishing miracle. The result was as significant and as satisfying to the farmer as the effect of myxomatosis when it cleared the rabbit from his cornfield and his pasture. The poisoned bait did everything its makers claimed for it. The old rat-catcher must have sighed as often as the man who had made his living catching rabbits and looked ruefully at his string of little Jack Russells, his traps and other gear. The farm rat was gone for good, it seemed. He had ruined his last sack of barley, cut his way under the last barn door, rolled away his last egg. The rat-catcher was redundant. As in the case of the miracle DDT, it was a long time before the poison seemed here and there to have less effect on a diminished rat population. DDT had ceased to be effective against flies in some parts of the world because some flies had resistance to the compound. The survivors seemed to have bred what was an apparently immune strain. It took about as long for the expert to spot the new rat. The newspapers called it the super rat. It was a high-sounding name for a survivor, a strain commonly encountered in every species of animal that lives on through setbacks and doesn't become extinct. There was no danger of the rat becoming extinct! The expert on genetics might have predicted what would happen, though it takes a very long time for the Warfarin-immune rats to prove the poison totally useless.

In an industry as important as agriculture—the production of meat and grain, to put it in its very simplest terms—the use of weedkillers, insecticides, fungicides and seed-dressings has become vital. There might have been a time when a balance could have been drawn between the effort made and the benefit accruing, the cost in terms of labour and material, and the profit from the crop. When it was accepted that chemistry and biology were the real science of agriculture and horticulture everyone was in the chemical business whether they liked it or not. There was no argument against an increase in production, a greater yield. Faddists might mumble about people dying from cancer or accumulated poisons of one sort or another but the poorer people of the world were dying of something just as terrifying—malnutrition.

The foot that presses on the accelerator is now the scientist's foot. He doesn't work for the farmer so much as for governments and the large chemical companies of the world. He has a great contempt for individuals who really don't know what they are talking about when they want to have no chemical warfare. A pest is a pest and war must be total. All wars cost a great deal of money and the ordinary man must pay for them. He must pay if he wants butterflies as well as corn. He must pay if he insists upon the insecticide being developed to cope with only a specified species and not every insect that climbs the same stalk. He must also pay if plants are to be bred free of the viruses that have hitherto made them unprofitable. The trouble in the case of pests and funguses is always in the soil. The treatment of the soil can go on for ever or the crop must be banned, the land left unplanted for as long as it takes to cleanse it.

There are other scientists, biologists, who look closer at the whole business of growing things and talk about making Hodge and his master totally redundant. Once again they would bring it all into the shed, like the bullock and the hen! They would have done with the machine on the field, the combine, the plough and the spraying tackle. The whole thing could be managed like a clinic simply by controlling temperature and light and gently feeding the soil-less roots of plants with a tepid solution of nutrients. There would be no fungus, no virus, not the sign of a beetle or an aphid in this vast clinic. The whole thing would be done under laboratory conditions. They have the plan and they toy with it more and more! A field of wheat without rust might be grown in vast plastic vats. Barley would never topple before the wind and the corn would never fail to ripen. There would be no loss. The man managing the plant would achieve his norm watching gauges, blending mixtures. It has already been done with lettuces and tomatoes. All that is needed is attention to techniques and a simplification of what is done in the laboratory. There is possibly one small drawback that no one cares to point out at his early stage. What will the nutrients cost and what price will the consumer pay for his loaf of bread if it is made from laboratory wheat? Already in another sphere of development the would-be fish farmer suggests that he can grow freshwater fish as good as the fish of the sea. He could farm all lakes, ponds, reservoirs and canals as well as the rivers of the country, and save the fisherman from the horrors of the North Sea in mid-winter or the wastes of the Arctic beyond! What would produce these fresh-water fish and make them grow as large as the wild fish of the sea but by feeding them pellets of protein? The old farming adage applies, a man must put something in to get something out! He will get a return on his labour and a certain return on whatever he spends to protect and safeguard his crop. He will have to put some-thing into the land. He must prevent its exhaustion but if he poisons his environment the chemist doesn't tell him how he can decontami-nate it. It is possible to measure up and put a price on all the chemi-cals that make up the human body but no chemist has ever reconsti-tuted anything! The biologist or pathologist might give us a larger wheat grain, a bigger potato, a giant pumpkin, an outsize stick of rhubarb. Perhaps the biologist can still solve our problem if he can persuade us to eat something else? In the end we may breed up immunized individuals who will not succumb to poisons, the accumulated effects of sprays and plant inoculations! The superman will survive like the super rat or the super fly. For the unfortunates with the wrong genes the only consolation may be that if they are not to starve to death, poisons generally have a slower effect than malnutrition. We may be able to point to the politician responsible for famine, but we can never identify a poisoner!

Away out on the moor a simple countryman looks at the bare tract of heather and wonders where the wheatears have gone and the insect-eating birds that were once so plentiful. He doesn't suspect that when the fleeces of his newly-dipped sheep are washed by the rain poison that killed the parasite in the fleece drains into the peat. There it has killed the insects. The birds never come back. Who is responsible? The man carefully making up the prescription in a laboratory hundreds of miles away from the heather! Tell him about it and he will say that he can make a safer one. It will cost a lot of money and take a decade. It is a pity we are all in such a hurry and have our foot so hard on the accelerator pedal!

EPILOGUE

F OR SOMETHING like two hundred years those concerned with the consequences of industrial development have looked with a certain dismay at the pattern of change in the nature of the countryside and the shift in population. The difficulty for most people seems to be in getting perspective on what is really happening. It has not been simply a case of the peasant uprooting himself and seeking the easier life of the city, for few men are more firmly set in their groove than the countryman. The peasant is redundant. The change in the countryside is an industrial one and the fondest dreams of the idealist can't put Hodge back on the land. It is true that we may reverse certain processes we have set in motion. We can, for instance, plough a field one year and make it a permanent pasture the year after. We can change the course of a motorway or close a railway. We can landscape where we delved for opencast coal and build a barrier across a river and all of these things will have some effect on what we have tomorrow. Nevertheless we influence evolution in no significant way. What we may achieve is too often governed by forces generated before we were born. The human race is not a regiment to be commanded to make an about turn or even persuaded to wheel even in the face of a recognizable enemy. The trickles and minor streams that run ahead of the flood are not to be diverted, and only in the world of pure fantasy can we contemplate car-workers, the stockbroker, the accountant and the salesman being persuaded back to the land. To employ even a small number of the 'lost countrymen' on the land would mean going back to old-fashioned methods. The land could never produce enough to feed their dependents. There is no room for people working manually.

The romantic is saddened to think that the picturebook world is disappearing. He shudders to think that Giles sits watching telly in a double-glazed, centrally-heated farmhouse with a whisky on the rocks by his elbow. He is whimsically encouraged at the thought that not every farmer enjoys such luxuries and misses the point that those who can't make the 'good life' are almost certainly doomed to extinction. Millais didn't paint this kind of world. He saw his sower striding lop-sidedly on the crumbling furrow scattering corn from a horny palm. Van Gogh and Bruegel saw a different world too, and perpetuated the romantic's dream with pictures of potato-eaters and potato-pickers. The world as it is is less satisfying to the sensitive soul. The modern picture is of an eighteenfoot swath cut by a giant combine rolling into an endless plain of wheat with not a peasant to be seen anywhere.

We can do about as much to arrest the seeming oncoming horror as Canute could do against the tide but the message is already there to be read. There was parkland unbroken where the motorway glides north. Hares once sat on the meadow where we built our city temples and kites that fed on offal perched on the gallows tree. Change had been a continual process since man himself came out of the trees. Along the way we have lost craft and gained technology. We have wrung the neck of the crowing cock, taken away the living of the village tailor and the weaver. We throw away our shoes without taking them to the cobbler and we have become convinced that what is wrong with the underdeveloped nation is that it ploughs with an ox. We can solve its problem as we have solved our own— if we really have solved our own—but there can be no standing still and no going back, even though someone may prove that we can still make fire by rubbing two sticks together or live on grass without becoming bloated. The danger we face is no greater than any we have faced in the past. We shall survive, either as an agricultural economy, or by some means which may ultimately make the farmer as redundant as the mower. The relics of the past are fascinating because when we look at them we learn so much about ourselves! In the horsepower age we are making relics faster than ever we did before. We hurry into tomorrow and tomorrow, but Shakespeare's words must be amended. This is no petty pace that creeps in from day to day. The blast-off is almost overpowering, and yet it is only the beginning. A whimsical clown says stop I want to get off. He should have asked before he was born.